Photoshop
Type Magic 2

D1304887

Photoshop Type Magic 2

BY GREG SIMSIC

Hayden
Books

Photoshop Type Magic 2

©1996 Hayden Books

Library of Congress Catalog Number: 96-77856
ISBN: 1-56830-329-7

Printed in the United States of America 1 2 3 4 5 6 7 8 9 0

Warning and Disclaimer

**President of Developer,
Technical and Graphics Group**
Richard Swadley

Associate Publisher
John Pierce

Publishing Manager
Melanie Rigney

Managing Editor
Lisa Wilson

Marketing Manager
Stacey Oldham

Acquisitions and Development Editor
Beth Millett

Production Editor
Kevin Laseau

Technical Editor
Gary Adair

Publishing Coordinator
Rachel Byers

Cover Designer
Aren Howell

Book Designer
Gary Adair

Manufacturing Coordinator
Brook Farling

Production Team Supervisors
Joe Millay
Regina Rexrode

Production Team
Trina Brown, Dan Caparo, Aleata Howard, Linda Knose,
Christopher Morris, Scott Tullis, Pamela Woolf

v

About the Author

Greg Simsic

Photoshop Type Magic 2 is Greg's second book, following his coauthorship of the successful *Photoshop Type Magic*. He has done freelance design work for the likes of BradyGAMES Publishing and DayDream, Inc. Greg holds a degree in the liberal arts from Ball State University and is currently a student of sculpture at Herron School of Art in Indianapolis. While not staring lovingly into his magic crystal computer monitor, Greg roams across the midwestern landscape looking for loose change.

Trademark Acknowledgments

All terms mentioned in this book that are known to be trademarks or service marks have been appropriately capitalized. Hayden Books cannot attest to the accuracy of this information. Use of a term in this book should not be regarded as affecting the validity of any trademark or service mark. Apple, Mac, Macintosh, and Power Macintosh are registered trademarks and AppleScript is a trademark of Apple Computer, Inc. Microsoft and Windows are registered trademarks and Windows NT is a trademark of Microsoft Corporation in the USA and other countries.

Dedication

This book is dedicated to the flowers next to my computer.

- Greg

Special Thanks to...

David, Becky, Michael, Rich, and Gary for making the first volume of *Photoshop Type Magic* a success and making this second volume possible.

Beth and the rest of the Hayden team for making the making of this book so easy.

Adobe for creating an application that allows my wandering mind a way to earn a living.

Hayden Books

The staff of Hayden Books is committed to bringing you the best computer books. What our readers think of Hayden is important to our ability to serve our customers. If you have any comments, no matter how great or how small, we'd appreciate your taking the time to send us a note.

You can reach Hayden Books at the following address:

Hayden Books
201 West 103rd Street
Indianapolis, IN 46290
317-581-3833

Email addresses:

America Online: Hayden Bks
Internet: hayden@hayden.com

Visit the Hayden Books Web site at `http://www.hayden.com`

Contents at a Glance

Introduction xiii
Before You Start 1
Photoshop Basics 5
Type Effects and Variations 18
Appendix A: Contributor's Listing 223
Appendix B: What's on the CD-ROM 229
Gallery 233

Contents

Introduction xiii
Before You Start 1
Photoshop Basics .5
Balls 18
Binary 24
Camouflage 28
Canvas 32
Carpet 38
Cereal 40
Checkered 44
Chrome (Airbrushed) 50
Clay 54
Confetti 58
Coral 60
Cotton 66
Decayed 72
Distressed 74
Fingerpaint 78
Foam 84
Foil 88
Fonts 90
Fur 96
Gold 100
Highlights 102
Icing 106
License Plate .112
Lights 114
Marble 120
Marquee Lights 122
Mosaic 126
Net 132
Paper Bag 138
Pinched 142
Plaid 144
Reflector 148
Scraps 152
Scribble 158
Shaping Text .162
Shimmering 168
Stained Glass .172
Stamped 180

Stones 186
Tiles 190
Tire Tracks 196
Torn Paper Edges 200
Waffle 206
Wallpaper 210
Watercolor 214
Woven 218
Appendix A: Contributor's Listing 223
Appendix B: What's on the CD-ROM 229
Gallery 233

Introduction

I just couldn't stop. I was fooling around on my Mac again, and out popped a few more type effects to keep you busy.

Perhaps you peeked in to see what's new. Unfortunately, there is nothing new. It's the same old, boring thing—great type that's easy to make. If you're just getting started with Photoshop, then do not fear—the special blue type radiates a magical field of power that will transform you into...no, no, no. The blue type refers you to special instructions in the Photoshop Basics section of the book. If you know your way around Photoshop then you can zip right through the uncluttered—but informative—steps that take you through techniques that will spur your own creative and technical forces into action.

Don't forget to check out all the stuff on the CD, keep brushing your teeth, and experiment, experiment, experiment! Oh, wait...toothpaste type. Hmmm... There's work to do. Gotta go. Happy typing.

Greg Simsic

Before You Start

Welcome

Welcome to this second volume of special type techniques for Adobe Photoshop users. More than a how-to manual—this book is a what-to guide. The steps in this book tell you exactly what you need to do in order to create exactly what you want. Flip through the alphabetized thumbtabs to find the type effect you want to create and follow the concise, explanatory steps. If you need a little extra help, flip to the "Photoshop Basics" section. But, before you jump into the type treatments, let me tell you a little about how this book works. A quick read now will maximize your time later.

System Setup

Here are the system recommendations for creating these type treatments.

Mac users: The Adobe Photoshop 4.0 Info box suggests a memory allocation of 21 megabytes (MB) of RAM to run Photoshop. And your system software may need as much as 10MB of RAM. That's a full bowl of soup, but if you've got the memory, then I would recommend setting the Preferred memory size even higher than 21MB. If you don't have 21MB to spare, then just quit all other applications and give it everything you've got. Generally, I give Photoshop 40MB of RAM.

PC users: Adobe suggests 32MB of RAM for Photoshop on any 386 or faster processor running Windows 3.1, Windows 95, or Windows NT, but 40MB is better. Quit any application you can before starting Photoshop to maximize the running of the application. Photoshop runs 32-bit native on both Windows 95 and Windows NT operating systems.

It is not crucial, but it will help if you have a CD-ROM drive. A number of the effects in this book use files that are contained on the CD that comes with this book. (See Appendix B, "What's on the CD-ROM," for information on accessing those files.) However, even if you don't have a CD-ROM drive, you still can perform all of the effects described in the book.

1

Adobe Photoshop 4.0

All of the techniques in this book were created with Adobe Photoshop 4.0, and that's the version I recommend you use. If you're attempting to duplicate these techniques using an earlier version of Photoshop, your results may differ slightly or significantly. If you're working with version 3.0, then you still will be able to create all of the effects in the book. However, keep in mind you will need to adjust the instructions for the differences between the two versions. You will see that even some of the old Photoshop features work differently in Photoshop 4.0. Most of the effects in this book use features that were not available in earlier versions of Photoshop.

Conventions

Every image in this book was created initially as a RGB file. You can make your effects in any appropriate color mode, but you should be aware of the variations this will cause as you proceed through the steps. For example, the first new channel created in an RGB file is automatically named Channel #4. But the first new channel created in a CMYK file is named Channel #5. You also should be aware of the differences in the color ranges of the various color modes. Some colors that look great in RGB mode may look like mud after you convert the file color mode to CMYK. **Note:** Quite a few techniques in this book use the Lighting Effects filter. This filter will not work in a CMYK or Grayscale file.

If you would like more detailed information about the different color modes, refer to a good general book such as *Adobe Photoshop Classroom in a Book*, or to your user manuals.

Also, every type image (except Fur) was created as a 5-inch by 2-inch, 150-dpi resolution file. (The thumbtab images were created as 300 dpi files.) If you are going to work in a resolution other than 150 dpi, remember that some of the filters and commands will require different settings than the settings I used. Because there are fewer pixels in a 72 dpi image, a Gaussian Blur radius of 5 pixels will blur the image more than if it were a 150 dpi image. Just keep an eye on the figures next to the steps and match the outcome as close as you can.

The Toolbox

For some of the effects, I used a third-party filter or a specially prepared preset file. Any of these extras tools that are not included with the standard Photoshop software are listed in the Toolbox in the lower-left corner of the first page of each technique. The Toolbox lists everything that you will need to create each type effect and any of its variations. The CD-ROM that comes with this book contains all the files needed to perform all of the basic techniques. For information on accessing these files, turn to Appendix B, "What's on the CD-ROM."

The Steps

The Blue Type

As you work through the steps, you will see phrases that are colored a light blue. These same phrases are listed in alphabetical order in the "Photoshop Basics" section. If the phrase in blue asks you to perform a task that you are unfamiliar with, then you can find that phrase in the "Photoshop Basics" section and follow the instructions on how to perform that task. Advanced users can perform the task as they normally would.

Menu Commands

You also will see instructions that look like this:

Filter➤Blur➤Gaussian Blur (2 pixels)

This example asks you to apply the Gaussian Blur filter. To perform this command, click on the Filter menu at the top of the screen and drag down to Blur. When Blur is highlighted a new menu opens to the right, from which you can choose Gaussian Blur.

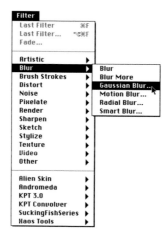

In this example, a dialog box appears asking you for more information. All of the settings that you need to perform each task appear in the text of the step. The previous example tells you to enter 2 pixels as the Radius.

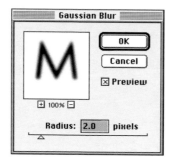

Click OK to blur the type.

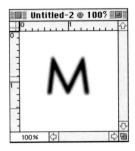

Settings

Following each action in the steps, you will find the settings for that feature. These recommended settings are meant to act as guides; the best settings for your type effect may vary. As a rule of thumb, it is best to match the outcome that you see in the figures as you progress through the technique. The greatest differences occur when the resolution of your file or the point size of your type are significantly different from what I used. The following two images demonstrate the importance of adjusting for resolution differences. A 6-pixel Radius Gaussian Blur was applied to both images.

75 DPI

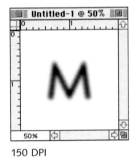
150 DPI

Tips

Throughout the book, you will find additional bits of information to help you render a better type effect. These tips provide information beyond the basic steps of each lesson. ■

Photoshop Basics

The goal of this section is to help new and novice users of Photoshop with the simple, basic tasks required to create the type effects described and illustrated in this book. Each of the basic tasks described in this section corresponds to the blue highlighted text in the chapters that follow. Here, users can easily find the instructions they need for performing a particular Photoshop task.

This chapter proceeds on two assumptions: that you're creating our type effects in Photoshop 4.0; and that you're keeping the Tool and Layer/Channel/Path palettes open. If one or both of the Tool and Layer/Channel/Path palettes are closed when you refer to this chapter, you can reopen them by name by using the Window menu at the top of the screen. If you're using an earlier version of Photoshop, you can refer to the Photoshop manual for instructions on how to perform these tasks. Also keep in mind that Photoshop 2.5 does not offer the capability to work in layers.

The Tools Palette

If you're not familiar with Photoshop's Tool palette, there's no reason to panic. With a bit of experimentation, it doesn't take long to learn each tool's individual functions. To help the beginning Photoshop user along the way, here is a representation of the toolbars from both Photoshop 3.0 and 4.0. This will also help advanced users find the rearranged tools.

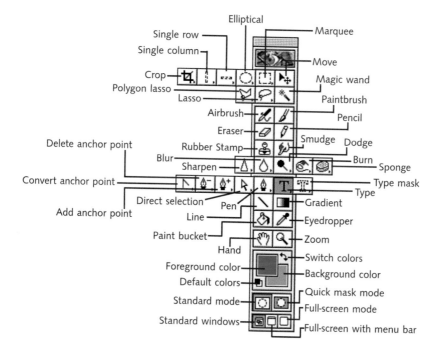

Photoshop 4.0 toolbar

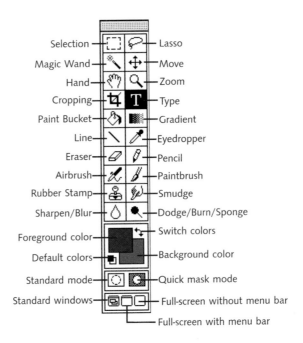

Selection — Lasso
Magic Wand — Move
Hand — Zoom
Cropping — Type
Paint Bucket — Gradient
Line — Eyedropper
Eraser — Pencil
Airbrush — Paintbrush
Rubber Stamp — Smudge
Sharpen/Blur — Dodge/Burn/Sponge
Foreground color — Switch colors
Default colors — Background color
Standard mode — Quick mask mode
Standard windows — Full-screen without menu bar
Full-screen with menu bar

Photoshop 3.0 toolbar

Basic Photoshop Tasks

Choose a Foreground or Background Color

Shortcuts: Press D to change colors to their defaults: black for the Foreground, and white for the Background.

Press X to switch the Foreground color with the the Background color.

To change the Foreground or Background color click on either the Foreground icon or the Background icon.

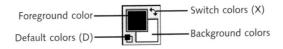

Foreground color — Switch colors (X)
Default colors (D) — Background colors

The Color Picker dialog box appears, which enables you to choose a new Foreground or Background color by moving and clicking the cursor (now a circle) along the spectrum box, or by changing specific RGB, CMYK, or other percentage values. Note that the Foreground and Background icons on the Tool palette now reflect your color choices.

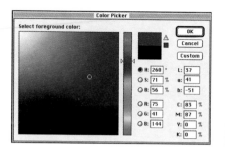
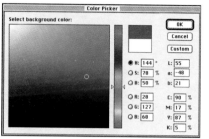

Convert to a New Mode

To convert from one color mode to another, click on the Image menu at the top of the screen and scroll down to the Mode selection. You then can scroll down to select the mode of your preference. For example, if you want to switch from CMYK mode to Multichannel mode, you choose Image➡Mode➡Multichannel. The checkmark to the left of CMYK will move down to Multichannel, indicating that you are now in Multichannel mode.

TIP
Remember that there is a different range of colors available for each color mode. No matter what color mode the file is in on-screen, for example, your printer (if it prints in color) is going to print your work in CMYK. Because the color ranges for RGB and CMYK are different, you should convert your RGB image to CMYK before printing. Otherwise, you may be in for a big surprise when your bright green prints as a dull tan.

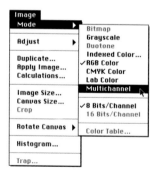

Create a Layer Mask

To create a layer mask, choose Layer➡Add Layer Mask, and choose either Reveal All (white) or Hide All (black). For the purposes of the effects in this book, always choose Reveal All. A layer mask is used to mask out (or hide) specified parts of a layer.

Create a New Channel

Shortcuts: Click the New Channel icon on the Channels palette.

To create a new channel, choose New Channel from the Channels palette pop-up menu.

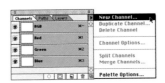

Use the Channel Options dialog box to establish your settings. Unless noted otherwise, we used the default settings when creating a new channel. This figure shows Photoshop's default settings.

Create a New File

Shortcuts: Press Command-N [Control-N].

To create a new file, choose File➞New. The New dialog box appears, which is where you name your new file and establish other settings. See Part I, "About this Book," for information on the conventions that were used when creating new files for the type effects in this book.

8

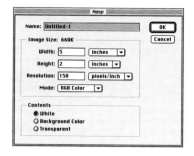

Create a New Layer

Shortcuts: Click the New Layer icon on the Layers palette.

To create a new layer, choose New Layer from the Layer palette pop-up menu, or choose Layer➡New➡Layer.

The New Layer dialog box opens, which is where you name the new layer and establish other settings.

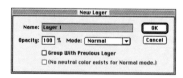

Delete a Channel

To delete a channel, go to the Channels palette and select the channel you want to delete; drag it to the Trash icon at the lower-right corner (just like you would to get rid of a document on the Desktop). You also can select the channel you want to delete, and choose Delete Channel from the Channels palette arrow menu.

9

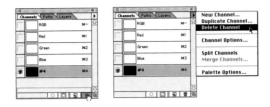

Deselect a Selection

Shortcut: Press Command [Control]-D.

To deselect a selection, choose Select➔None. The marquee disappears.

Duplicate a Channel

Shortcut: Click the channel you want to duplicate, and drag it on top of the New Channel icon.

To create a duplicate of a channel, make the channel active and then select Duplicate Channel from the Channels palette pop-up menu.

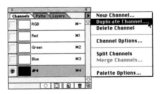

A new copy of the channel you selected for duplication is created automatically, and the Duplicate Channel dialog box appears.

Enter/Exit Quick Mask

Shortcuts: Press Q to enter and exit the Quick Mask mode.

Click the Quick Mask icon to switch to Quick Mask mode; conversely, click the Standard mode icon to return to Standard mode.

Essentially a Quick Mask is a temporary channel. When you're in Quick Mask mode you can use any of the Photoshop tools and functions to change the selection without changing the image. When you switch back to Standard mode you'll have a new selection.

Enter the Text

There are two Type tools in Photoshop 4.0; the standard Type tool and the Type Mask tool. Each effect in this book specifies which type tool to use.

Before entering the text using the standard Type tool, make sure that the foreground color is set to your desired text color. Often, the instructions in this book ask you to enter text into a channel. Unless noted otherwise, it is assumed that you are entering white text onto the black background of the channel. If you are entering text into a layer, then the standard Type tool will create a new layer for the type.

The Type Mask tool creates selection outlines of the text you enter without filling the outlines with a new color, and without creating a new layer.

To enter the text, select the type tool that you want to use, and then click anywhere in the image to open the Type Tool dialog box. Type the text in the large box at the bottom of the dialog box, and make your attribute choices from the options (listed previously). Unless noted otherwise in the instructions, always make sure that you have the Anti-Aliased box checked.

11

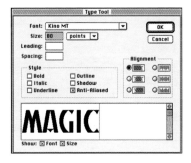

After clicking OK, move the type into position with the Move (standard Type tool) or Marquee (Type Mask tool) tool.

Fill a Selection with Foreground or Background Color

First, select the Foreground or Background color you wish to use (see page 6 in this section for instructions). Keep the selection active and press the Option-Delete keys to fill the selection with the Foreground color. If you are in the Background layer or any layer that has the Preserve Transparency option turned on, then you can press Delete to fill in the selection with the Background color.

You also can fill in your selections by choosing Edit➞Fill.

This causes the Fill dialog box to appear, allowing you to establish the Contents option you wish to use, the Opacity, and the blending Mode.

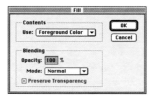

TIP If a selection is empty (a transparent area of a layer) and the Preserve Transparency option is turned on for that layer, then you will not be able to fill the selection. To fill the selection, simply turn off the Preserve Transparency option before filling it.

Flatten an Image

To flatten an image (merge all the layers into a single layer), choose Flatten Image from the Layers palette arrow menu, or choose Layer➞Flatten Image.

Load a Selection

Shortcut: Hold down the Command key and click on the channel (on the Channels palette) that contains the selection you want to load.

To load a selection, choose Select➤Load Selection. This brings up the Load Selection dialog box, where you can establish document, channel, and operation variables.

 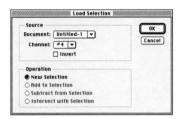

Load the Transparency Selection (of a Layer)

To load the transparency selection of a layer, hold down the Command key and click on the layer (on the Layers palette) that contains the transparency selection you want to load.

Make a Channel Active

To make a channel active for editing or modification, click on its thumbnail or title on the Channels palette.

13

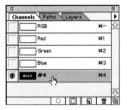

You can tell the channel is active if it is highlighted with a color.

Make a Layer Active

To make a layer active, click on its thumbnail or title in the Layers palette.

You can tell the layer is active if it is highlighted with a color.

Make a Layer Visible/Invisible

To make a Layer visible, click in the left-most column in the Layers palette. If an eye appears, then the layer is visible. If the column is empty, then that layer is hidden (invisible).

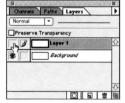

Move a Layer

To move a Layer, click on the layer you want to move in the Layers palette and drag it up or down the list of layers to the place you want to move it. As you drag the layer, the lines between the layers will darken to indicate where the layer will fall if you let go.

The layer you moved will appear between layers—numerically "out of order."

Return to the Composite Channel

Shortcut: Press Command-`.

If you want to return to the composite channel, click on its thumbnail or title (RGB, CMYK, Lab). The composite channel always will be the one with Command [Control]-~ after its title.

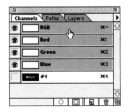

If you are in an RGB file, then Channels 0 through 3 should now be active because each of the R, G, and B channels are individual parts of the RGB channel.

Save a File

To save a file, choose File➡Save As. This displays the Save As dialog box, where you name your new file and choose a format in which to save it.

File format selection depends on what you have in your file, what you want to keep when you save it, and what you're going to do with the file after it is saved. Consult a detailed Photoshop book, such as *Adobe Photoshop Classroom in a Book*, for more guidance on which file format is best for your needs.

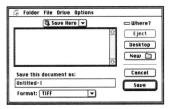

15

Save a Selection

Shortcut: Click the Save Selection icon on the Channels palette.

To save a selection, choose Select➥Save Selection.

The Save Selection dialog box opens. Choose your options and click OK to save the selection.

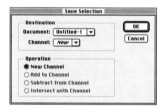

Switch Foreground/Background Colors

Shortcut: Press X to switch the Foreground and Background colors.

To switch the foreground and background colors, click on the Switch Colors icon. This flips the two colors shown in this icon only, and does not affect the rest of the image.

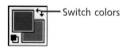
Switch colors

Switch to Default Colors

Shortcut: Press D to switch to the default foreground and background colors.

To change the foreground and background colors to black and white respectively, click on the Default Colors icon.

Default colors

Turn On/Off Preserve Transparency

To turn on or off the Preserve Transparency option for a particular layer, first make that layer the active layer. Then, click the Preserve Transparency checkbox on the Layers palette. This option is not available for the Background layer. ∎

Follow the bouncing balls, or rather the numbered steps, to create a shaded sphere onto which you can lay type.

1 Create a new file. Click the Marquee tool on the Tools floating palette to select it. You can scroll through the different Marquee tools by holding down the Option [Alt] key and clicking on the current Marquee tool. Find the Elliptical Marquee.

2 With the Marquee tool, draw a circle. If you hold down the Shift key while dragging the Marquee, the selection will be constrained to a perfect circle.

3 Change the foreground color to a color for the ball, and the background color to the color for the shadow. You can use white for the ball but I wanted to add a little color, so I used the CMYK values 4, 1, 51, 0, for the ball and black for the shadow.

4 Double-click the Gradient tool to select it and to display the Gradient Tool Options floating palette.

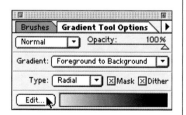

5 Fine-tune the gradient for the ball. First, click the Type pop-up menu and change the Type to Radial. Also, make sure that the Gradient is set to Foreground to Background.

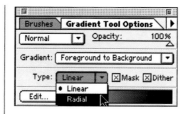

Then click the Edit button (as shown in the previous figure). A new dialog box will appear. Click the tab in the lower left that has an "F" inside it. Then click the pointer just below the colored gradient above. Drag the new "F" marker until the Location box reads 22%.

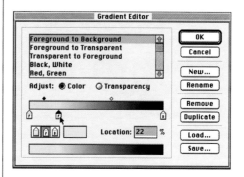

Grab the diamond above the colored gradient, which is to the right of the marker you just placed. Drag it to the right until the Location box reads 62%. Click OK.

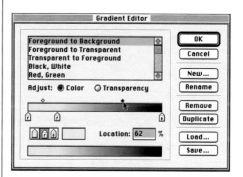

6 Now, back to the circle selection. Click and drag the Gradient tool from the upper left part of the active selection to the lower right part of the selection as shown here.

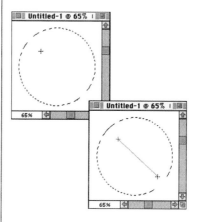

19

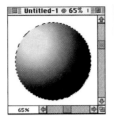

Here's what I got. If you don't like what you get, press Command-Z [Control-Z] and repeat this step.

7 Change the foreground color to a color for the type. I used black. Then use the Type tool to enter the letter for the ball. I used 55 point Palatino. The type will drop automatically into a new layer (Layer 1). Position it in the center of the sphere, and deselect the type.

8 Get the elliptical Marquee tool and draw a perfect circle around the number that is smaller than the ball behind it. Something similar to this will do.

9 Next, choose Filter➡Distort➡ Spherize (Normal), and slide the amount to the maximum. I applied the filter a second time (Command-F) [Control-F]. Flatten the image and you're finished.

VARIATIONS

Off-Center

You don't have to keep the letter in the middle of the ball. After you type it in, just drag it to the spot where you want it and continue with the steps described earlier.

Highlights

After flattening the layers, you can add a highlight that will blend the letter onto the ball better. Change the Foreground color to white. Double-click the Gradient tool and use the settings that you see here.

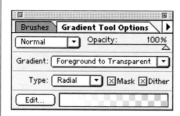

This is what you get.

Here's another way to make glossier balls. Perform Steps 1 through 3, except in Step 3 make the Foreground color white and the Background color black. You can do this by pressing D, and then X. The ball selection should still be active. Do Steps 4, 5, and 6, and make a new layer and name it Color. Keep the selection active. Change the foreground color to a color for the ball, and press the Option-Delete keys to fill the selection. The gradation disappears. From the pop-up menu on the Layers palette change the mode to Color. There is your shiny ball. Complete Steps 7 through 9 to add the text.

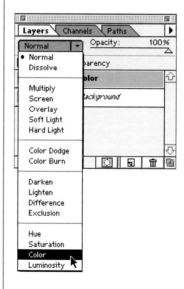

21

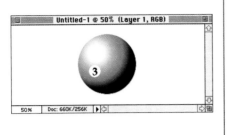

Untitled-1 @ 50% (Layer 1, RGB)

50% Doc: 660K/256K

Billiards

Now turn that ball into a billiards ball. I used Method 2 for this variation. After finishing Step 6, make a new Layer and select the Elliptical Marquee tool again. Click and drag a perfect circle on top of the ball. Change the foreground color to white and fill the selection.

Do Steps 7 through 9. In Step 8, I drew the Marquee selection to match the outline of the ball. Here is how the type turned out. ∎

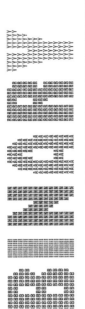

How retro! First we will make a guide for the type with large letters, then build the letters one at a time.

1 Create a new file. Use the Type tool to enter the text. Use a basic, sans serif, hard-edged font like Helvetica for this type that will serve as the guide for the individual letters. I used Impact at 90 points. The type will drop automatically into a new layer (Layer 1).

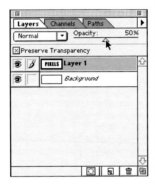

2 Use the Opacity slider on the Layers palette to lower the opacity of Layer 1 to 50%.

3 Make a new layer (Layer 2). Then make the Background layer and Layer 1 invisible.

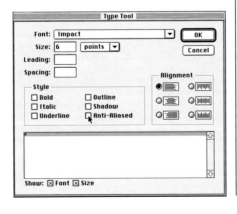

4 Use the Type tool to enter the first letter of the word you typed in Step 1. Make the type about 15 times smaller than the type you chose in Step 1. The letters probably will be so small (6 points in my case) that you will want to turn off Anti-Aliasing. However, be careful that the letters remain intact, because turning off Anti-Aliasing can trim them down.

5 Select a box around the letter with the Marquee tool. Leave just a little room around the letter, like this.

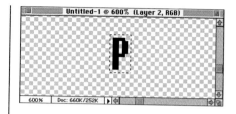

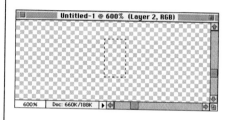

TIP When working with type this small, it helps to zoom in. Use the Zoom tool to enlarge the image. (In this example, I have zoomed in to 600% in order to make a more accurate selection.)

6 Choose Edit➤Define Pattern to define the selected letter as a pattern. Press Delete to get rid of the letter.

7 Make Layer 1 visible again. Hold the Command [Control] key and click on the Layer 1 preview on the Layers palette to load the type selection.

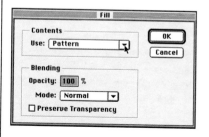

8 Change the foreground color to black. Make Layer 2 active, and choose Edit➤Fill. Click on the Contents pop-up menu and choose Pattern. Keep the Opacity set at 100%, and the Mode set at Normal.

Now you can see how the small type size you chose in Step 3 works inside the type you entered in Step 1.

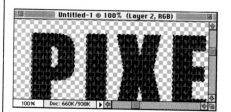

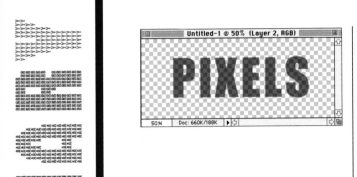

9 Press Command-Z [Control-Z] to undo the fill. If the small type size does not look right inside the larger type, then go back and enter the text again in Step 3. If the space between the letters is too much, then you probably selected too much area around the type in Step 4. Go back to Step 3 and try it again.

10 After you have established the right size and spacing for the letters, then select the Marquee tool. Drag a rectangle around the first letter like this.

11 Choose Edit➤Fill and use the same settings you used in Step 8.

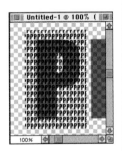

12 Select the Move tool and use the arrow keys to move the letters into a convenient location (so they fit nicely, or as nicely as you can get them) over the Layer 1 type.

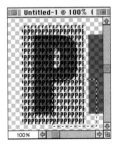

13 When satisfied, deselect the type. With the Marquee tool drag rectangles around the letters that you want to take away, like this:

After making several selections and deleting their contents, you should end up with something like this.

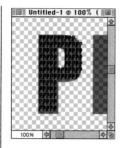

 You will probably have to make some judgment calls about which letters to delete and which to keep. The best rule is to be consistent with all the letters.

14 Deselect the letters. Make Layer 1 invisible again. Use the Type tool to enter the next letter at the same point size in an undefined area of Layer 2.

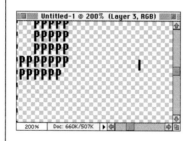

15 Perform Steps 5, 6, and 7. Make Layer 1 visible again. Then do Steps 11 through 14.

16 Continue this routine until all of the letters are complete. Remove Layer 1 when you are finished. Then flatten the image.

27

VARIATIONS

After removing Layer 1 in Step 16, hold the Command [Control] key and click the Layer 2 preview on the Layers palette to select all the letters of all the letters. Then choose Filter➤Noise➤Add Noise (Amount: 100; Distribution: Gaussian). Applying this filter adds the colored noise that you see in the thumbtab image. ■

In this effect, the Crystallize and Median filters work together to separate the text into flat areas of color—just what the camouflage needs.

1 Create a new file. Change the foreground color to these CMYK values: 81, 31, 100, 16. Fill the image with this color.

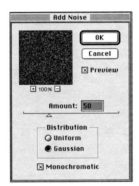

2 Choose Filter➤Noise➤ Add Noise. Turn on the Monochromatic option and keep the Amount low. (I set the Amount at 50.)

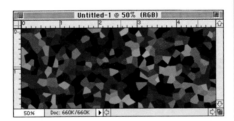

3 Choose Filter➤Pixelate➤ Crystallize. This filter divides the text into flat color areas. (I used a Cell Size of 30.)

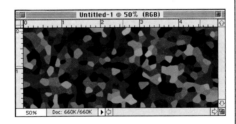

4 To finish creating the color shapes, choose Filter➤Noise➤ Median. Use a low setting, such as 5, which is what was used here.

5 Next, use the Type Mask tool to enter the text. This font is Incised Black at 90 points.

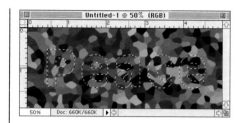

6 Choose Select➔Inverse. Then press Delete to fill everything with white, except the type.

7 Choose Select➔Inverse again. Then press Command [Control]-J to copy the type into a new layer (Layer 1).

8 Choose Filter➔Stylize➔Find Edges.

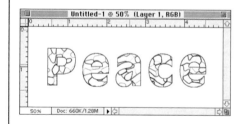

9 Then choose Image➔ Adjust➔Threshold. Slide the marker all the way to the right, until the Level reads 255.

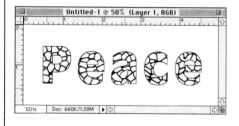

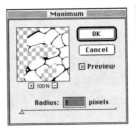

10 Choose Filter➡Other➡Maximum. This filter thins down the black lines. Use the minimum setting, 1 pixel.

11 Next, choose Layer➡Layer Options. Inside the Blend If box, grab the white This Layer slider and drag it to the left just a little—until the indicator above lowers to about 251.

Click OK and your type should now look like this. ■

What's great about this canvas type is that you can use the same technique to create many different textures. And, it's all done with the Paintbrush tool—and some help from the Lighting Effects filter.

1 Create a new file, and a new channel (#4).

2 Double-click the Paintbrush tool to select it, and to bring forward the Paintbrush Options dialog box. Click the Brushes tab to bring the brushes to the front. Then, click the Brushes arrow menu and choose Load Brushes.

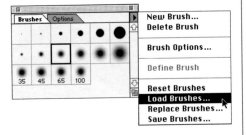

3 A dialog box opens so that you can find the brushes file that you want to use. Just for you, I have made a special brush to help create this texture. Actually, I modified one of Photoshop's Assorted Brushes. Follow this path to open the Magic Brushes file: Photoshop Type Magic 2➤Type Magic Presets➤Magic Brush. Open the file.

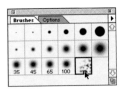

4 The Brushes palette now should include a new brush. Select the new brush.

5 Double-click the new brush to open the Brush Options dialog box. Change the Spacing to 50%.

TOOLBOX

Canvas (Lighting Style Preset)

6 Change the foreground color to white. Click in the image area and drag the brush.

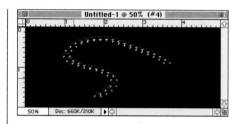

7 Go crazy rubbing the brush all over the image. Keep in mind that you are creating a texture—don't obliterate the black. I used a circular motion when creating this texture, seen here in a close-up.

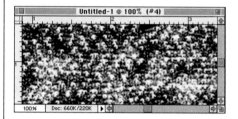

8 To finish the texture, choose Filter➤Pixelate➤Fragment.

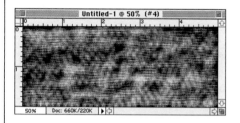

9 Return to the composite channel and make the Background layer active. Use the Type Mask tool to enter the text. I used Attic at 85 points.

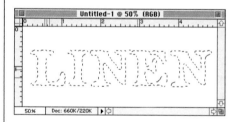

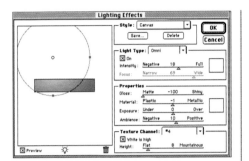

10 Choose Filter➤Render➤ Lighting Effects. If you have loaded the Lighting Style presets from the CD, you can select Canvas from the Style pop-up menu or match the settings you see here.

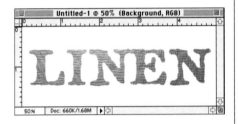

11 Choose Filter➤Noise➤Add Noise. Turn on the Monochromatic option, but don't overdo the noise. I set the Amount to 30. The texture may have looked a little plastic, adding noise will give the texture a more natural look.

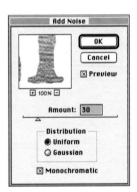

34

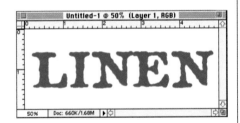

12 Keep the selection active and make a new layer (Layer 1). Change the foreground color to a color for the type, and fill the selection in Layer 1.

13 Convert the Layer 1 blending mode to Color.

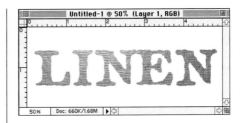

VARIATIONS

Instead of filling the Layer 1 selection with a flat color in Step 11, I used the KPT Gradient Designer. I chose the Multi Color nonlinear preset gradient. Now do Step 12.

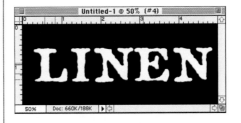

How do you create the rough edges as seen on the thumbtab? Follow the steps described below.

After Step 1, use the Type tool to enter the text into Channel #4. Deselect the text.

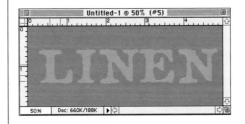

Then create a new channel (#5). Keep Channel #5 as the active channel, but make Channel #4 visible as well.

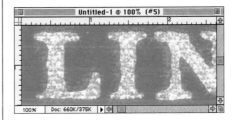

Change the foreground color to white. Then, select the same brush shown in Step 4 above. Paint over the letters. Be sloppy, but not too sloppy. You want something like this:

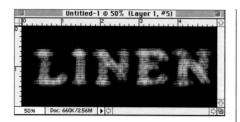

Follow the instructions in Step 8, and then duplicate Channel #5 to create Channel #5 copy.

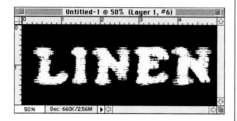

Choose Image➔Adjust➔ Threshold. Use the slider to set the Level close to 80. The shape of the white area will be the shape of the type.

Return to the composite channel, and load the selection Channel #5 copy. In the Lighting Effects dialog box, in Step 10, change the Texture channel to Channel #5. Do Steps 11 and 12. ■

This quick effect takes advantage of the Accented Edges filter—one of the new Brush Strokes filters in Photoshop 4.0. Using the right settings in this filter is the key to creating the carpet texture.

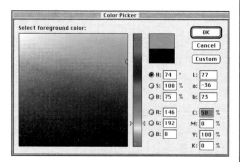

1 Create a new file. Use the Type Mask tool to enter the text. Benguiat Bold at 120 points was used for this example.

2 Change the foreground color to a color for the carpet. I used these CMYK values: 50, 0, 100, 0. Fill the selection with this color.

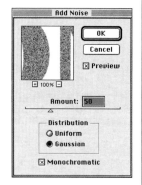

3 Save the type selection to create Channel #4.

4 While keeping the selection active, choose Filter➔Noise➔Add Noise. Set the Amount at a value just under the point at which white pixels show up in the pre-view. I set the Amount at 50. (Gaussian, Monochromatic). Deselect the text.

5 Next, choose Filter➔Brush Strokes➔Accented Edges. This filter can create many varied effects, but to create the carpet texture match the setting as seen here (Edge Width: 1, Edge Brightness: 22, Smoothness: 2).

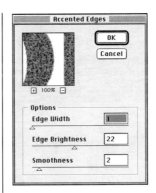

Your type will have a texture like this:

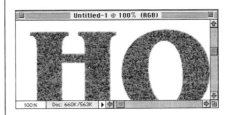

6 Apply the Accented Edges filter again, but raise the Edge Brightness to 23.

7 Load the selection you saved in Step 3 (Channel #4). Then choose Select➔Modify➔Contract. Contract the type selection 1 pixel.

8 Finally, choose Filter➔Pixelate➔Fragment. Here's a detail of the texture...

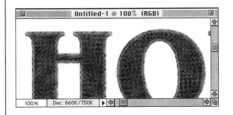

...and here is the final type. ■

The unlikely Ocean Ripple filter works with the Lighting Effects filter to round out these crunchy letters.

1 Create a new file, and a new channel (#4). Use the Type tool to enter the text. Font choice for this effect is important. I used Thickhead (100 points) because the shapes of the letters look like bulbous Cheerios.

2 Save the selection to create Channel #5. Keep the text selection active.

3 Choose Filter➡Distort➡Ocean Ripple. This is one of the new filters from Photoshop 4.0. Try these settings to distort just parts of the type: Ripple Size: 1; Ripple Magnitude: 13.

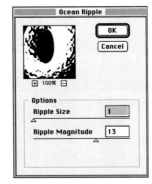

 TIP If the word you typed is too long, the Ocean Ripple filter may distort some of the letters too much. If this happens, try selecting only a few of the letters at a time, and apply the filter. Continue until the Ocean Ripple filter has been applied to all the letters. Then load the selection Channel #5 to select all the letters again.

4 Next, choose Filter➡Blur➡ Gaussian Blur. Blur the text enough to smooth out the distortion created by the Ocean Ripple filter. I set the Radius at 8.8.

TOOLBOX

Cereal (Lighting Style Preset)

5 Create a new channel (#6). The selection should still be active. Choose Filter➤Pixelate➤ Mezzotint. Select the Coarse Dots option from the pop-up menu.

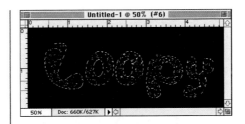

6 Make Channel #4 active, then load the selection Channel #6.

7 Choose Image➤Adjust➤ Brightness/Contrast. Lower the Brightness value to about -35. Deselect the selection.

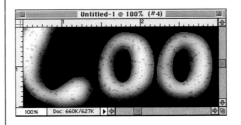

8 Load the selection Channel #5. Choose Filter➤Noise➤Add Noise (Gaussian). Set the Amount to around 4. The noise helps create some shallower bumps in the cereal letters, but keep it low.

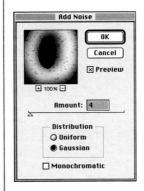

9 Return to the composite channel. Keep the selection active.

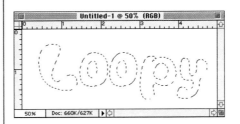

41

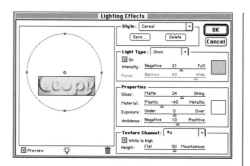

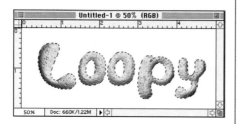

10 Choose Filter➡Render➡ Lighting Effects. Choose the Cereal preset from the Style pop-up menu, or match the settings in this figure. Use the Texture Channel Height to adjust the full-ness of the letters.

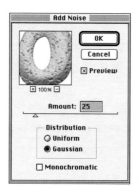

11 As a final touch, I chose Filter➡Noise➡Add Noise and low-ered the Amount to 25. This noise will give the cereal texture a little graininess, and we all know how important grain is to our diets.

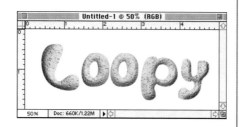

VARIATIONS

I just couldn't resist adding this milky background and a shadow.

If you have a hard-edged font that you want to round off for this effect, follow these steps.

In Step 1, use the Type Mask tool instead of the Type tool. This font is Impact at 100 points.

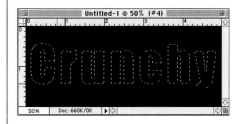

Then choose Select➟Modify➟ Smooth. You may have to try different settings before you get the one you want. I smoothed the selection 10 pixels.

Fill the selection with white and finish the steps above (Steps 2 through 11).

If you're looking for a change from your everyday breakfast type, try Waffles (page 206). ∎

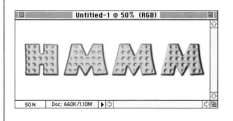

43

Making a checkered pattern takes only a few steps. Once you've got that down, you can use Photoshop's filters to make some unique alterations.

1 Create a new file, and a new layer (Layer 1). Change the Foreground color to one of the colors you want to use for the checkers, and fill the entire layer with the color. I used the CMYK values 24, 24, 98, and 16.

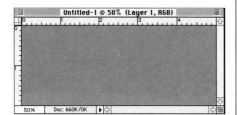

2 Double-click the Marquee tool to select it and to bring the Marquee Options floating palette to the front. Change the style to Fixed Size, and set the Width and Height to 10 pixels. These dimensions determine the size of the squares in the checkered pattern. Adjust it to your liking, but make sure you always keep the Width and Height the same.

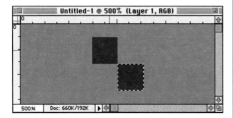

3 Next, click in the image area once with the Marquee tool. A square selection appears. Change the Foreground color to the second color for the checkers. I used the CMYK values 99, 70, 7, and 1. Fill the selection with this color.

4 Use the Marquee tool to move the selection so that the upper-left corner of the selection meets the lower-right corner of the colored square that you created in Step 3. Fill this selection with the same color that you used in Step 3.

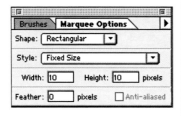

5 Find the Marquee Options floating palette again, and double the Width and Height sizes (20 pixels for me).

6 Use the Marquee tool to click in the image area. Drag the new, larger, square selection so that it includes both of the colored squares.

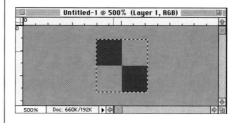

7 Choose Edit➺Define pattern and then choose Select➺All. Press Delete to clear the image window. Deselect the selection.

8 Use the Type Mask tool to enter the text. I used Frutiger Ultra Black at 90 points.

9 Choose Edit➺Fill. In the dialog box, change the Contents option to Pattern. Click OK, and you've got checkers.

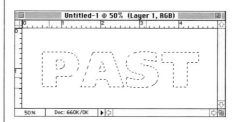

Diagonal Checks

Do Steps 1 though 6 above, and then choose Layer➺Transform➺ Numeric. The only setting you need to change is the angle. Change it to 45°.

45

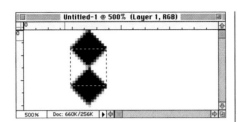

Again, find the Marquee Options floating palette. Change the style to Constrain Aspect Ratio and make sure that the Width and Height settings are changed to 1. This option keeps the selection a perfect square. Drag the Marquee to make a selection like this:

When you finish Steps 7 through 9, your type should look like this.

VARIATIONS

Keep the type selection active after Step 9, and make a new layer (Layer 2). Use the Gradient tool to fill the type selection with the Yellow, Violet, Orange, Blue preset gradient. Then change the Layer 2 mode to Color.

Or, change the layer mode to Difference.

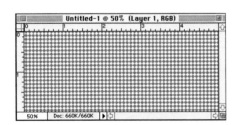

Skip Step 8 above, and follow the instructions in Step 9. The entire layer (Layer 1) should fill with checkers.

Then choose Filter➡Brush Strokes➡Crosshatch and use these settings: Stroke Length, 3; Sharpness, 9; Strength, 3.

Now do Step 8. Choose Select➡Inverse and press Delete.

Try these settings for the Crosshatch filter for a different effect: Stroke Length, 13; Sharpness, 20; Strength, 3.

To make plaid text that is a little different from the technique on page 144, use these settings in the Crosshatch filter: Stroke Length, 9; Sharpness, 5; Strength, 3.

Try applying the same filter again, but this time use the original settings: Stroke Length, 3; Sharpness, 9; Strength, 3.

For these variations, first I made the checkered type in channels. You can do this by creating a new file, and a channel (#4). Then start with Step 2 above. In Steps 3 and 4, fill the selections with white. Skip Step 8, so the entire

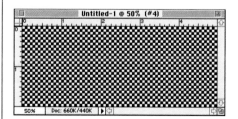

47

channel fills with the checks. I started by making these two channels. Channel #4:

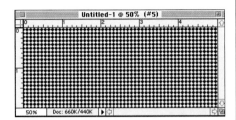

and Channel #5.

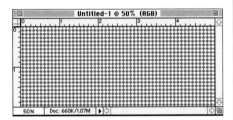

Return to the composite channel and load the selection Channel #5. Choose a foreground color and fill the selection.

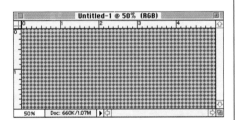

Choose Select➔Inverse. Choose another foreground color and fill the selection.

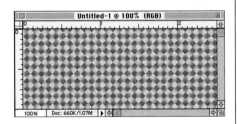

Then load the selection Channel #4 and choose Filter➔Blur➔ Gaussian Blur. I set the Radius at 2.3 pixels, but you can use this setting to create a variety of differrent patterns. Find something you like and move on.

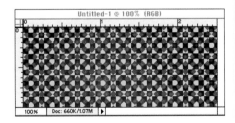

That is an interesting effect by itself. Try changing the foreground color again and choosing Filter➔ Render➔Difference Clouds.

You can repeat the last step as many times as you want.

Then do Step 8 on page 45. Choose Select➡Inverse and press Delete. ■

Airbrushed chrome is one of the old standby type effects. It is quick and easy to create, but Photoshop 4.0 has made it even easier to create with its new custom gradients feature.

1 Create a new file, and a new channel (#4). Use the Type tool to enter the text into this new channel. For this effect, I used Poplar-Laudatio at 110 points.

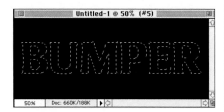

2 Create another new channel (#5). The selection should still be active.

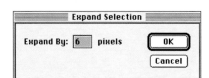

3 Choose Select➞Modify➞ Expand. The number you enter here determines the width of the metallic border. I expanded the selection 6 pixels.

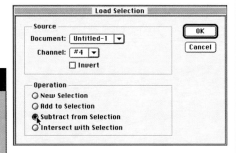

4 Next, load the selection Channel #4, with the Subtract from Selection option turned on.

TOOLBOX

Chrome (Lighting Style Preset)

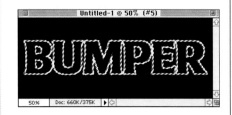

5 Fill the selection with white.

6 Return to the composite channel. The thin border selection should be active. Again, choose Select➤Modify➤Expand (2 pixels).

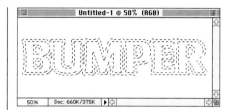

7 Choose Filter➤Render➤Lighting Effects. This filter raises the border slightly. Choose Chrome from the Style pop-up menu or match the settings in this figure, which are not much different from the default values.

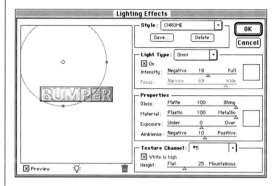

The type should now look like this.

8 Load the selection Channel #4. Double-click the Gradient Tool icon to display the Gradient Tool Options floating palette. As mentioned earlier, one of the great new features of Photoshop 4.0 is that you can define your own gradients. For those of you familiar with making custom gradients in Adobe Illustrator, Photoshop's custom gradient feature is very similar.

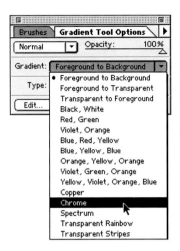

Click the Gradient pop-up menu and choose—you guessed it—Chrome. This is your lucky day. Adobe Photoshop includes a pre-set Chrome gradient.

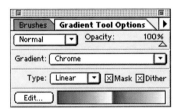

Match the rest of the settings to what you see in this figure.

9 Hold down the Shift key and click the Gradient tool inside the type, near the top of one of the letters. Then drag straight down (holding the Shift key forces the line to remain straight) to the bottom of the letters.

Now that was easy.

VARIATIONS

You can adjust the preset Chrome gradient if it's not quite right for your effect. Drag the middle markers to change where the two gradients meet; or click one of the markers to highlight it. Then click the color box below and choose a new color for the blend. I changed the Chrome gradient as you can see in this figure...

...and got this.

This effect is just begging for some highlight sparkles. Flip to page 102 to learn an easy way to put them on your type. ■

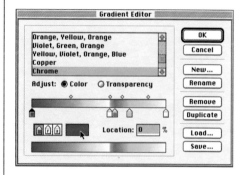

53

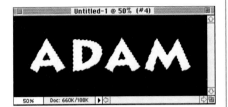

For this effect you will create a texture channel to be used by the Lighting Effects filter.

1 Create a new file, and a new channel (#4). Use the Type tool to enter the text. The type in this example is Lithos Black at 80 points.

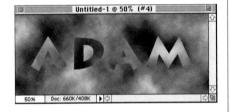

2 Save the selection to create Channel #5. Deselect the type.

3 Then choose Filter➔Render➔ Difference Clouds to fill the channel (#4).

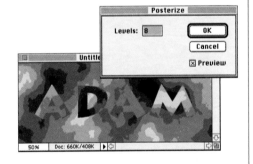

4 Choose Image➔Adjust➔ Posterize. Keep the setting low. I used 8 levels. This step flattens the cloud gradation into flat areas that look like scraped clay.

54

TOOLBOX

Clay (Lighting Style Preset)

5 Then choose Filter➔Render➔ Difference Clouds, again. This is the channel that will be used for the clay texture.

6 Return to the composite channel, and load the selection Channel #5. Choose Select➔ Modify➔Expand (2 pixels). Expanding the selection eventually gives the type its lip.

7 Choose Filter➔Render➔Lighting Effects. You can choose Clay from the Style menu or match the settings in this figure.

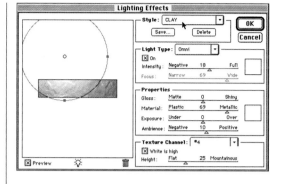

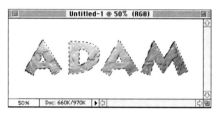

8 Keep the selection active and choose Image➔Adjust➔Auto Levels.

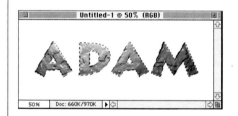

9 Then choose Image➔Adjust➔ Hue/Saturation. Check the Colorize box and try these settings:

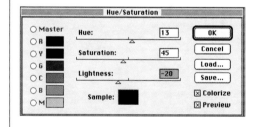

Deselect the text.

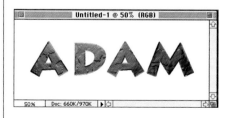

VARIATIONS

Adding Cracks

To add cracks, follow the previous steps with these exceptions:

After Step 5:

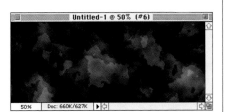

5(a) Create a new channel (#6). Choose Filter➔Render➔ Clouds. Then choose Image➔ Adjust➔Posterize (8 levels), and Filter➔Render➔Difference Clouds. Look familiar?

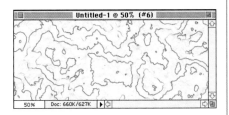

5(b) Next, choose Filter➔ Stylize➔Find Edges.

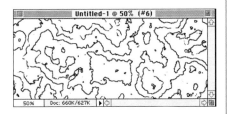

5(c) Then choose Image➔ Adjust➔Threshold. The slider can be used to control the heaviness of the clay cracks. The threshold level for this example was set at 223.

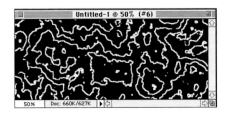

5(d) Press Command-I [Control-I] to invert the channel. Then choose Filter➔Other➔Maximum (1) to widen the white lines.

56

5(e) Make Channel #4 the active channel and load the selection Channel #6, with the cracks you just made. Fill the selection with black.

6(a) Do Step 6, then load the selection Channel #6 and check the Subtract from Selection option in the Load Selection dialog box. You should have a selection like this.

Complete the rest of the steps, and you should end up with an effect that looks something like this. ■

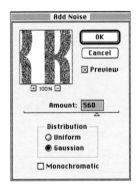

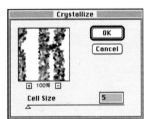

The Noise and Crystallize filters team up to do most of the work for this effect.

1 Create a new file. Use the Type Mask tool to enter the text. I used the Birch font at 90 points. Choose black for the foreground color and fill the text selection.

2 Choose Filter➤Noise➤Add Noise. Slide the marker to the right until most of the black pixels are replaced by colored pixels. For the desired effect in this example, the marker was moved until the amount hit 560. Deselect the text.

3 Then choose Filter➤Pixelate➤Crystallize. In the preview you will see the noise pixels turn into flakes (the greater the Cell Size, the larger the flakes). Just make sure that you still can read the text. Here's how the text looks with a Cell Size of 5.

4 Now, we need to get rid of all the blacks and grays. Choose Image➔Adjust➔Selective Color. From the Colors pop-up menu choose Blacks. Then slide the black marker all the way to the left (-100%). Do the same for the Neutrals and Whites categories. You will see all the blacks and grays disappear from your text.

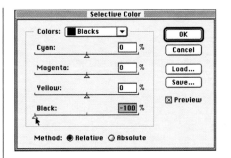

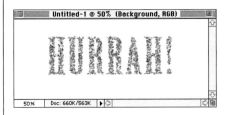

5 Now to control that glaring color, choose Image➔Adjust➔ Replace Color. Oh no—so many controls! Just relax and play. Use the Eyedropper to click on a color in the image window. All similar colors will be selected. The Fuzziness slider control allows you to expand the selection to include more similar colors. With the Hue, Saturation, and Lightness sliders you can change the color you selected. When you are satisfied with the first color change click OK. Then repeat this step to change the next color. ■

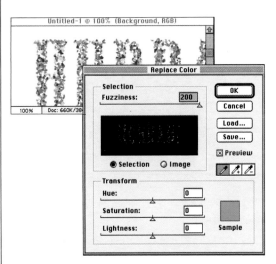

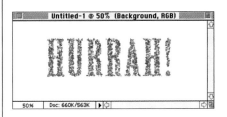

59

One of the new Sketch filters in Photoshop 4.0, Reticulation, allows you to create this coral effect. This filter produces just the right texture that you can coax into becoming coral.

1 Create a new file, and a new channel (#4).

2 Choose Filter➡Sketch➡ Reticulation. The settings in this filter do not have to be precise. Just to make it easy though, I entered 20 for all three variables.

3 Choose Image➡Adjust➡Invert. Now you can see the beginning of the coral pattern.

4 You may need to enlarge the pattern for your type. To do this, select the rectangular Marquee tool and drag a selection, like this:

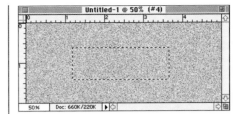

5 Then choose Layer➔Free Transform. Grab the corners of the box and drag them toward the corners of the image window.

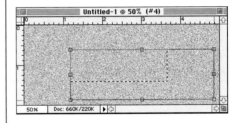

Press the Return [Enter] key to accept the changes.

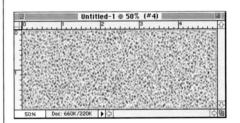

6 Choose Image➔Adjust➔Levels. The graph in the Levels dialog box shows a large mound piled up on the right side. Grab the left (black) marker and slide it to the right until it is under the beginning of this mound.

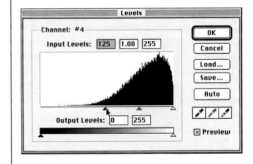

61

You are looking for something like this:

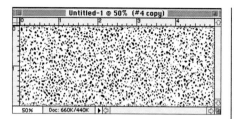

7 Duplicate Channel #4 to create Channel #4 copy. Then choose Image➞Adjust➞Threshold. Set the Threshold Level near 76. This channel, along with Channel #6 (created in Step 9), will be used to set the outlines of the wriggling coral.

8 Return to the composite channel and make a new layer (Layer 1). Then use the Type Mask tool to enter the text. I used the Bauhaus font at 120 points.

9 Save the selection to create Channel #6.

10 Then load the selection Channel #4, with the Intersect with Selection option turned on.

Load Selection

Source

Document: Untitled-1

Channel: #4

☐ Invert

Operation
○ New Selection
○ Add to Selection
○ Subtract from Selection
◉ Intersect with Selection

OK

Cancel

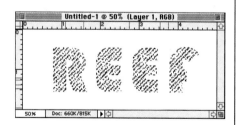

11 Change the foreground color to white and fill the selection. You won't see any change on the screen because the Background layer is visible and is filled with white.

12 Make another new layer (Layer 2), and move the new layer below Layer 1.

13 Now load the selection Channel #6 (the channel that contains the type selection). Then load the selection Channel #4 copy with the Intersect with Selection option turned on.

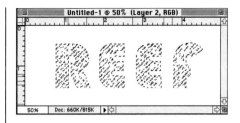

14 Change the foreground color to black and fill the selection.

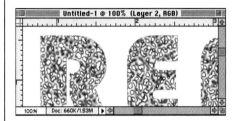

15 Make a duplicate of Layer 2 to create Layer 2 copy. Then move Layer 2 copy above Layer 1.

16 Change the blending mode for Layer 2 copy to Color. It will appear as though the black has disappeared.

17 Choose Image➤Adjust➤Hue/Saturation. Turn on the Colorize option. Raise the Lightness and use the Hue and Saturation markers to choose a color for your coral type.

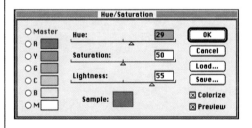

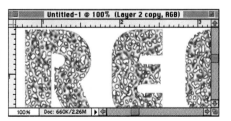

63

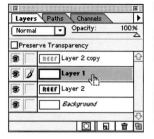

18 To work on the texture, make Layer 1 the active layer, and load the transparency selection of Layer 1.

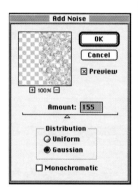

19 Choose Filter➤Noise➤Add Noise. I kept the Monochromatic option unchecked. Choose Gaussian and set the Amount at 155. Try other settings to produce slightly different textures.

Click OK and you're finished. ■

This effect involves a little channel work to create some fancy selections that will fluff up your type.

1 Create a new file, and a new channel (#4). Use the Type tool to enter the text. I used Impact at 90 points. Save the selection to create Channel #5.

2 Choose Select➪Modify➪ Contract. Contract the selection so that it shrinks to about one-third of its width. I chose 6 pixels. Save the selection to create Channel #6.

3 Again, choose Select➪ Modify➪Contract. Contract the selection to the same amount as in Step 2. Save the selection to create Channel #7.

4 Load the selection Channel #5, and then load the selection Channel #7 with the Subtract from Selection option turned on.

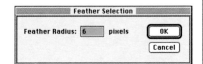

5 Choose Select➪Feather. Feather the selection to about the same amount as you contracted it in Step 2. All of the feathering you do in this technique helps to make sure that the texture is soft.

6 Choose Filter➔Noise➔Add Noise (Gaussian). Add a low to medium amount of noise. Just make sure that you add less noise in Step 8. I set the Amount at 140 pixels.

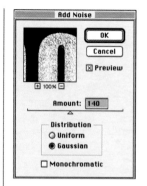

7 Choose Filter➔Pixelate➔ Crystallize. Use a low Cell Size. I chose 6 pixels. In the preview, you should see some rockiness appear among the noise. Keep the rocks small.

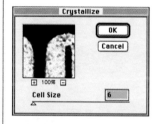

8 Choose Filter➔Noise➔Add Noise again. Add a little less noise (about 100 pixels).

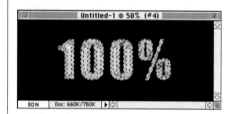

9 Choose Filter➔Noise➔Median (1 pixel) to smooth out the noise a little.

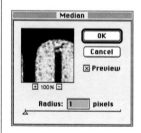

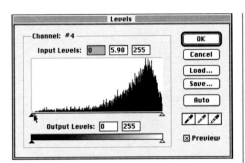

10 Choose Image➤Adjust➤Levels, and grab the middle (gray) marker and slide it all the way to the left.

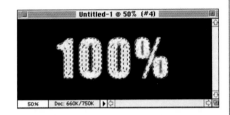

You now are about halfway through this effect and your type should look something like this.

11 Now let's run through this same routine one more time. Load the selection Channel #5, then load the selection Channel #6 with the Subtract from Selection option turned on. Choose Select➤Feather and feather the selection about half as much as you did in Step 5.

12 Do Steps 7 through 9 with this new selection.

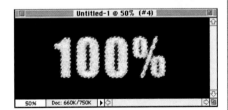

13 Load the selection Channel #4 (the same channel that you should be in).

14 Choose Image➤Adjust➤Levels, grab the middle (gray) marker and slide it all the way to the left. (This is the same thing you did in Step 10.)

15 Return to the composite channel. Make a new layer (Layer 1), then make another new layer (Layer 2).

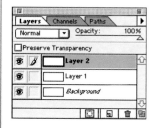

16 Change the foreground color to white and load the selection Channel #4. Fill the selection with white. Nothing will happen in the image window because you just filled white on white. But you will see the effect in a few steps.

17 Make Layer 1 the active layer. Change the foreground color to black. Fill the selection.

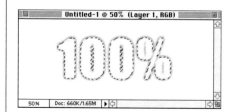

18 Select the Move tool and use the keyboard arrow keys to move the shadow (Layer 1) two keystrokes to the right, and two keystrokes down.

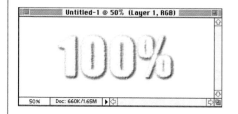

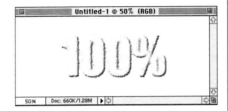

19 Deselect the text. Choose Image➤Adjust➤Threshold. Slide the marker to the left, watching the preview until you get something that looks like this. Flatten the image and you're finished. ∎

For this effect, you first need to break up the edges of the type, and then use the Lighting Effects filter to raise the interior of the type.

1 Create a new file, and a new channel (#4). Use the Type tool to enter the text into the new channel. A font with serifs (prey for our decaying techniques) works well. I used Sabon at 120 points for this example.

2 Deselect the type, then choose Filter➤Pixelate➤Crystallize. This filter will roughen the edges. Keep the Cell Size small so that the interiors of the letters remain intact. For this example, I set the Cell Size to 10.

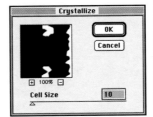

3 Choose Filter➤Blur➤Gaussian Blur, and blur the type just a little. I chose a Radius of 2.

> **TIP** With smaller type, the blurring may not be necessary.

4 Next, choose Filter➤Stylize➤ Diffuse (Normal).

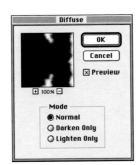

5 The decaying has begun. The more times you apply this filter, the more the type will break up. The larger the type, the more applications it will take to break it up. After the filter was applied 20 times, the text channel looked like this:

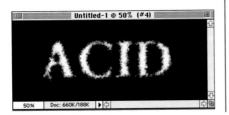

72

TIP If you want to reapply the last filter that you used with the same settings, press Command-F [Control-F].

6 Return to the composite channel, and load the selection you just created (Channel #4).

7 Change the foreground color to a color for your type. I used the CMYK values 16, 8, 69, 2. Fill the selection with the color.

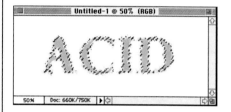

8 Choose Filter➤Render➤Lighting Effects. In the Lighting Effects dialog box you can click the Style menu and find the Decay preset or just match the settings seen in this figure.

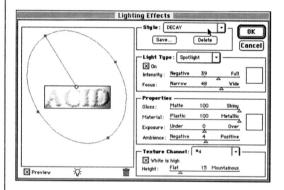

9 Deselect the type, and you're finished. ∎

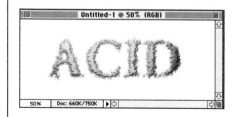

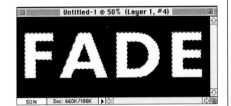

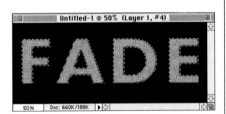

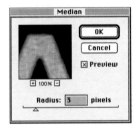

This effect runs through a number of filters, but the Clouds filter gives this effect the realistic touch it needs.

1 Create a new file, a new layer (Layer 1), and a new channel (#4). Use the Type tool to enter the text in the channel. It is helpful to use a thick font that can disappear in places and still be readable. In this example, I used Humanst at 120 points.

2 Next, choose Filter➤Pixelate➤ Pointillize and select the smallest possible Cell Size: 3.

3 Choose Filter➤Pixelate➤ Fragment.

4 Deselect the text, and choose Filter➤Noise➤Median. In this example, I used a Radius of 3 pixels.

5 To increase the contrast in this channel, choose Image➔Adjust➔ Levels. Look at the figure here to see the settings that were used.

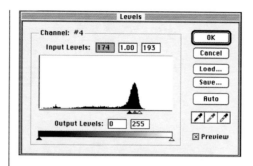

You can vary the settings, but watch the preview to make sure you get something similar to what you see in this figure.

6 Next, choose Filter➔Sharpen➔ Sharpen.

7 Make a copy of Channel #4 to create Channel #5. In Channel #5, choose Image➔Adjust➔Levels. Slide the middle Input triangle all the way to the left. Don't touch the others.

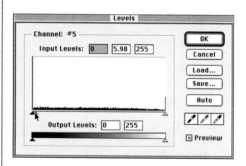

The channel should look like this:

8 Return to the composite channel, and make Layer 1 the active layer. Load the selection Channel #5. Change the foreground color to a color for the type, and fill the selection. I used the CMYK values 17, 98, 100, and 4, in this example.

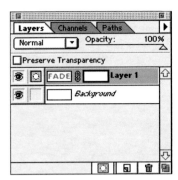

9 Choose Layer➤Add Layer Mask➤Reveal All to add a clear Layer mask to Layer 1. The Layers palette should look like this:

10 The heavy black border around the preview of the Layer mask means that it is the active area. Also, the selection still should be active. Choose Filter➤Render➤Clouds. The red type will dim.

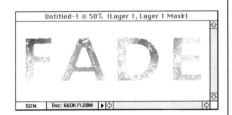

11 Next, choose Image➤Adjust➤Levels. Slide the black marker to the right until most of—but not all—the type fades away. The image preview should look something like this:

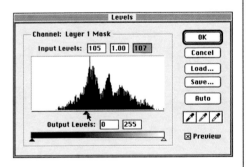

Then grab the right (white) marker and slide it to the left until all three markers line up on top of each other, like this:

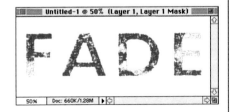

Your type should now look similar to this:

12 Click on the Layer 1 preview to make it active. The black box will switch from the Layer mask to the Layer preview.

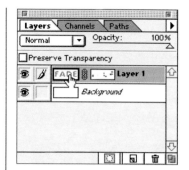

13 Finally, load the selection Channel #4 and choose Image➤Adjust➤Hue/Saturation. Click on the Colorize checkbox and use the sliders to add depth to the color. Here are the settings used for this example.

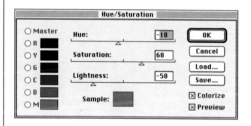

That's all there is to it.

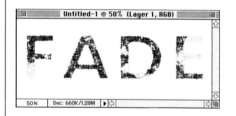

VARIATIONS

A Quick Method

Create a new file. Change the foreground color to white, and use the Type tool to enter the text. It will be placed into a new layer (Layer 1), but you won't see anything until you do the next step (since you have put white text on a white background). Perform Steps 2 through 6, then use the Hue/Saturation dialog box as described in Step 13 above. ∎

Among the many new filters Adobe has included with Photoshop 4.0 is the Ocean Ripple distortion filter. It comes in handy here for creating this messy type.

1 Create a new file. Use the Type Mask tool to enter the text. This font is Britannic Bold at 110 points. Fill the text with black.

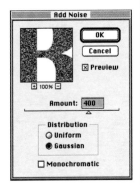

2 With the type selection still active, choose Filter➤Noise➤Add Noise. Raise the Amount to approximately 400.

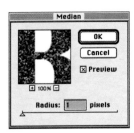

3 Deselect the type. Choose Filter➤Noise➤Median (1 pixel).

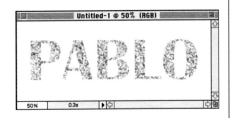

4 Then choose Filter➤Other➤ Maximum (2 pixels). You should have something that looks like this:

5 Choose Image➤Adjust➤Hue/
Saturation and turn on the
Colorize option. Then use the Hue
slider to find a color for your type.
I set the Hue slider at 38.

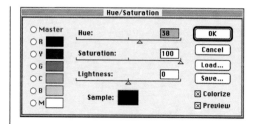

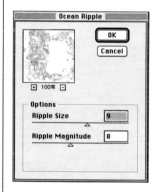

6 Now for the Ocean Ripple.
Choose Filter➤Distort➤Ocean
Ripple. I set the Options to Size:
9, and Magnitude: 8. This filter
will smear the noisy type.

79

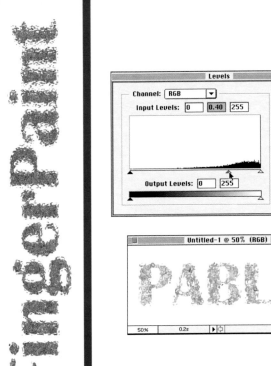

7 You may want to raise the contrast or add some darker colors to the type. Choose Image➡Adjust➡ Levels and slide the middle (gray) marker to the right.

VARIATIONS

While in the Levels dialog box in Step 7, slide the black marker to the right—until the Input indicators look like this:

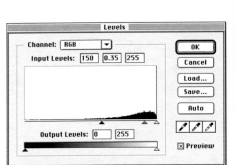

I call this "cheese pizza" type.

Who would fingerpaint in monochrome type? Follow these steps to add color(s) to the type.

1 Follow the steps above to create the first color. Before deselecting the type in Step 3, save the selection to create Channel #4.

2 Make a new layer, and fill the layer with white. Load the selection Channel #4, and fill it with black.

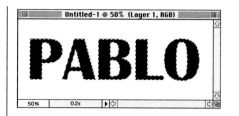

3 Complete Steps 2 through 7 as described above.

4 While the new layer is active, choose Layer➤Layer Options. Hold the Option [Alt] key and grab the left half of the white slider that is below the This Layer gradation. The triangle will split in half. Drag the left half to the left to about 150.

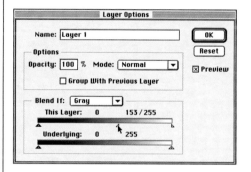

5 Do the same for the Underlying Layer slider.

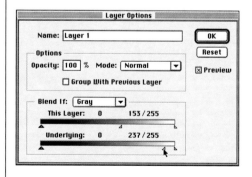

You can add as many colors as you want. Just keep repeating the last four steps. This image has four colors.

The layers' blending modes were changed to come up with these two variations. ∎

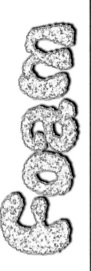

Here's the companion to the Tiles effect (page 190). To make it happen, two selection channels were made with basic filters.

1 Create a new file, and a new channel (#4). Use the Type tool to enter the text. I used Thickhead at 100 points. Add some spacing so the foam has room to lather. I set the spacing at 5.

2 Keep the selection active, and choose Filter➥Noise➥Add Noise. Add a medium amount of noise to break up the interior of the text. I set the Amount at 240.

3 Deselect the type, and choose Filter➥Stylize➥Diffuse. This filter starts spreading out the type.

4 Reapply the same filter to your heart's content, and watch the type squirm as it sprays pixels into the black. I applied the Diffuse filter eight times.

5 Duplicate this channel to create Channel #4 copy.

6 Choose Filter➛Blur➛Gaussian Blur. All you want is a slight fuzziness. I blurred the channel with a Radius of 0.5.

7 Return to the composite channel, and load the selection Channel #4.

8 Choose Select➛Feather. Again, just a small amount. I chose 1 pixel.

9 Change the foreground color to a color for the foam. The foam will end up white, but this color will be the tint that you see in the Foam example. I used the CMYK values 100, 75, 0, 40.

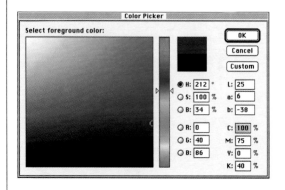

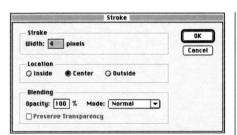

10 Choose Edit➤Stroke. Match these settings...

...and click OK.

11 Next, load the other selection Channel #4 copy.

12 Change the foreground color to white and fill the selection.

VARIATIONS

If you want a whiter interior, then keep the selection active after Step 12, and choose Image➤ Adjust➤Brightness/Contrast. Raise the Brightness to +100.

To add a little more color, keep the selection active after Step 12 and make a new layer (Layer 1). Choose a foreground color and fill the selection.

Then change the Layer 1 mode to Color.

Try the other modes, too. This one has the same color, but I changed the Layer 1 mode to Hard Light and lowered the Opacity to 25%.

Now, try Color Dodge (Opacity: 50%).

If you want more contrast, then deselect the type and choose Image➡Adjust➡Levels. Drag the left (black) Input marker to the right. You should get something like this. ■

TOOLBOX

Foil (Lighting Style
Preset)

Gold (Lighting
Style Preset)

This effect might be the quickest
in the book, thanks to the
Lighting Effects filter.

1 Create a new file, and a new
channel (#4). Use the Type tool to
enter the text. For this effect, I
used 110-point Matrix.

2 Keep the selection active and fill
it with clouds by choosing
Filter➔Render➔Clouds.

3 Return to the composite
channel. Keep the type selection
active, and choose Filter➔
Render➔Lighting Effects. If you
have loaded the Lighting Styles
presets from the CD, you can
choose Foil from the pop-up Style
menu. Otherwise, match the settings seen in this figure.

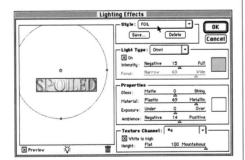

4 To brighten the foil, choose
Image➔Adjust➔Brightness/
Contrast and slide the Contrast
marker to +40.

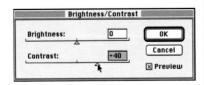

5 Ready for wrapping.

6 You also can use the new Polygon Lasso tool to draw a jagged selection.

Press Delete to give your type some teeth.

VARIATIONS

It's easy to turn this foil into gold leaf. In the Lighting Effects dialog box, just click on the color square in the Light Type box, and change the CMYK values to 25, 16, 71, 6 (or simply choose Gold from the Style menu).

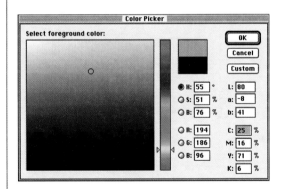

89

Here are a few simple ways to quickly transform basic fonts into something unique.

1 To begin each of the variations below, create a new file and use the Type Mask tool to enter the text. The type you end up with largely depends on the type you start with. This effect was started with 90-point Agaramond Bold. Change the foreground color to a color for the text, and fill the type selection.

The Maximum Filter

Slim the type down with the Maximum filter. Deselect the type, then choose Filter➤Other➤Maximum. As you increase the Radius in the dialog box the type shrinks more and more. Try a Radius of 4.

Here's another one you can make with the Maximum filter. I used Avant Garde Bold at 90 points in Step 1. Select the Marquee tool and move the selection (not the type) two keystrokes to the right and two keystrokes down.

Then choose Filter➔Other➔ Maximum (6 pixels).

Follow the instructions in Step 1 (using Humanst521 Bold at 85 points), then choose Select➔ Modify➔Contract (4 pixels).

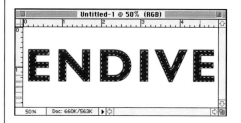

Select the Move tool and use the arrow keys to move the inside of the type. I moved the selection one keystroke down and two keystrokes left.

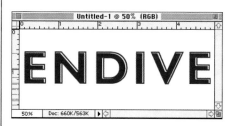

You can continue to alter this effect. I selected the Marquee tool and moved the selection back to its original place. Then I selected the Move tool and moved the selection contents again in the same direction.

And again.

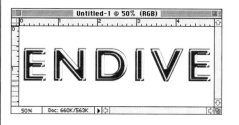

Displace

Follow the instructions in Step 1 (using Helvetica Condensed Black at 120 points). Deselect the type.

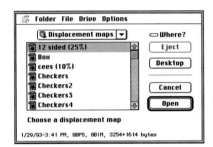

Now choose Filter➤Distort➤ Displace. I used 10% for both the Horizontal and Vertical Scales. Select Stretch to Fit.

When asked to find a displace-ment map, follow this path: Adobe Photoshop 4.0➤Plug-ins➤Displacement Maps. Choose the 12-sided file for some minor edge tweaking.

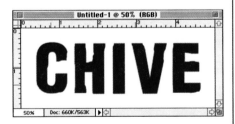

Several of the other Displacement maps have a similar effect on the type. For something different, change the Horizontal and Vertical Scale settings to 5, and choose the Fragment Layers file as the dis-placement map.

Posterize

Do Step 1 (using Bremen Bold at 85 points), and deselect the type. Then blur it by choosing Filter➤ Blur➤Gaussian Blur (Radius: 8).

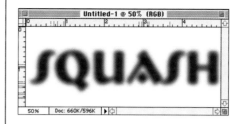

Then choose Image➤Adjust➤ Posterize (3 levels) to divide the type into three flat areas of color.

You can add one more step by choosing Filter➤Stylize➤Find Edges to get this outlined type.

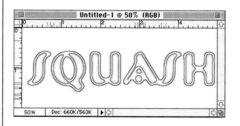

More quick alterations...

Do Step 1 again (using Agaramond Bold at 90 points). Keep the type selected and choose Filter➤Blur➤Gaussian Blur (about 6 pixels). Deselect the type and choose Image➤Adjust➤Threshold. Set the Threshold Level to reduce and smooth your type. I set it at 120.

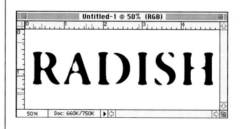

Before deselecting the type above, save the selection to create Channel #4. After using the Threshold feature, load the selection Channel #4, and choose Filter➤Stylize➤Wind (Blast, From the Left).

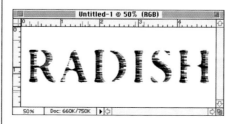

93

Follow the instructions in Step 1 (using Bodega Sans Black at 100 points). Deselect the type. Choose Filter➔Pixelate➔Fragment, and then choose Filter➔Noise➔Median (9).

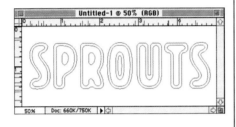

After creating the previous effect, apply Filter➔Stylize➔Trace Contour (Upper, 125).

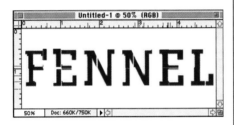

Perform Step 1 and use City Medium at 95 points. Then, choose Filter➔Stylize➔Tiles (Number of Tiles: 2; Maximum Offset: 10%).

Do Step 1 (using Badger Bold at 120 points). Deselect the type, and try one of the Brush Strokes filters, for example Spatter: Filter➔Brush Strokes➔Spatter (Spray Radius: 16; Smoothness: 9). ■

A combination of filters sets up the Motion Blur filter to make a short-haired type effect.

1 Create a new file, and a new channel (#4). Choose Filter➥ Render➥Clouds to fill the channel with clouds to start the texture.

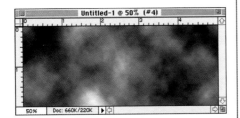

2 Choose Filter➥Noise➥Median (7 pixels) to smooth the clouds.

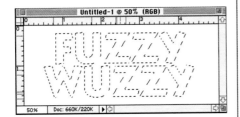

3 Return to the composite channel, and use the Type Mask tool to enter the text. I used 80-point Kabel.

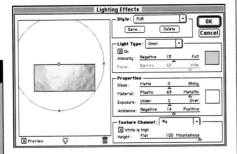

96

Fur (Lighting
Style Preset)

4 Choose Filter➥Render➥Lighting Effects. Use the settings as shown in this figure. If you loaded the preset files from the CD, then you can choose Fur from the Style pop-up menu. The light color in the Light Type box is going to determine the color of the fur. If you want something different from what I used, then change it now.

5 Keep the selection active, and choose Filter➡Other➡Minimum (7 pixels). The Minimum filter adds some contrast and helps create some spots in the texture.

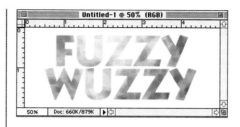

6 To read just the middle values, choose Image➡Adjust➡Levels. Grab the middle (gray) slider and drag it to the right, until the center Input Levels hits .60. Then slide the white marker to the left, just a little, to about 240.

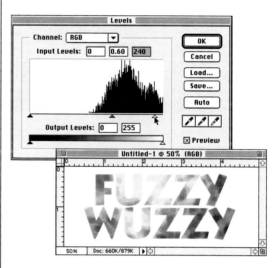

7 Now, add a little noise: Filter➡Noise➡Add Noise (12 pixels). Make sure the Monochromatic box is checked.

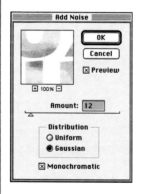

8 Then choose Filter➡Blur➡ Motion Blur. Use the settings as shown here (Angle: 50; Distance: 5). It is just a short blur to make the hairs.

97

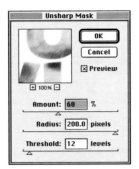

9 Choose Filter➤Sharpen➤ Unsharp Mask. Try these settings: Amount: 68%, Radius: 200 pixels, and Threshold: 12.

10 A black stroke helps this type stand out from the background. Choose Edit➤Stroke (2 pixels; Center: 100%, and Normal). ■

These steps are similar to the Foil effect, but the effect is created by using the same commands in a different order. If you want to make gold leaf, then flip to the Foil section on page 89.

1 Create a new file, and a new channel (#4). Fill the channel with clouds by choosing Filter➤Render➤Clouds.

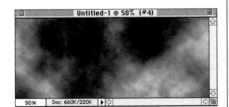

2 Choose Filter➤Noise➤Median. I chose 7 pixels. You will not see much effect on the clouds; however, this filter will meld the field of clouds into like areas.

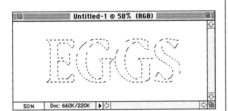

3 Return to the composite channel. Use the Type Mask tool to enter the text. I used Matrix at 130 points for this effect.

100

TOOLBOX

Gold (Lighting Style Preset)

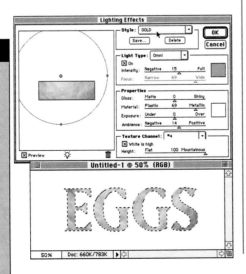

4 Keep the type selection active, and choose Filter➤Render➤ Lighting Effects. If you have loaded the files from the CD, then choose Gold from the Style pop-up menu; otherwise match the settings seen here.

5 Keep the selection active and choose Filter➞Other➞Minimum (7 pixels).

6 Then Choose Image➞Adjust➞ Brightness/Contrast and slide the Contrast marker up until your type looks like my final image here. I set the Contrast to +40. Deselect the text.

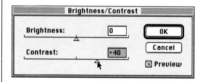

That's it.

VARIATIONS

To change the golden eggs to copper, keep the selection active and make a new layer. Double-click the Gradient tool to select it and bring to the front the Gradient Tool Options floating palette. Choose the Copper custom gradient from the Gradient pop-up menu. Click and drag the Gradient tool across the type selection in any direction. Then from the Layers palette menu change the Layer 1 mode to Hue. ■

EGGS

Here are three quick ways to add a sparkle to your type—plus a fourth method, courtesy of Andromeda's Star filter.

The Custom Paintbrush

1 Open the file containing the type you want to add highlights to. This type was created with the Chrome (Airbrushed) effect on page 50.

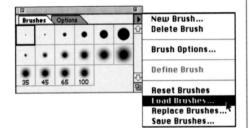

2 Double-click the Paintbrush tool to select it and to bring the Paintbrush Options floating palette to the front. Click on the Brushes tab to make the brushes palette active. Then choose Load Brushes from the arrow menu.

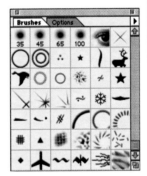

3 Follow this path to open the Assorted Brushes file: Adobe Photoshop 4.0➡Goodies➡Brushes & Patterns➡Assorted Brushes. A range of new brushes will appear in the Brushes palette.

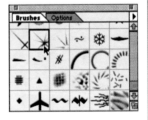

4 Scroll to the bottom of the palette and select this brush:

> **TIP** You can use the brushes on either side of the brush I recommended for slightly different sparkles.

102

TOOLBOX

Andromeda's
Star Filter

5 Choose white for the foreground color.

6 To add sparkles to the type, use the Paintbrush tool to click on the type where you want the sparkle. Don't drag the brush or you will smear the sparkle.

Sparkles, sparkles, sparkles.

 To intensify a sparkle, click twice on the same spot.

The Lens Flare

1 For this method, I started with this type created using the Reflector effect (page 148).

2 Choose Filter➔Render➔Lens Flare. In the dialog box preview, drag the flare to a spot on the type. I set the Brightness at 151%. Just make sure that the Brightness percentage is not so high that you have all highlight and no type.

Click OK and you're finished.

103

The Gradient Highlight

1 This type was created using the Balls effect on page 18.

2 Choose white for the foreground color, or another color for the highlight.

3 Double-click the Gradient tool to select it and to bring the Gradient Tool Options floating palette forward. Change the Gradient to Foreground to Transparent and the Type to Radial.

4 Click on the Edit button, then click on the Transparency button. Grab the black marker and slide it to the right a little. Then grab the diamond on top and slide it to the left a little. Click OK.

5 Click and drag with the Gradient tool from the point for the center of the highlight. Drag the Gradient line until it reaches as far as you want the highlight to spread.

Andromeda's Star filter

If you have Andromeda's Star filter, then you've got one more way
to add a highlight to your type.
There is a demo version of this filter on the CD. See page 230 to
find out how to access it.

1 I made some Stained Glass type
for this filter (page 172).

2 Choose Filter➡Andromeda➡
Star. The dialog box enables you
to control every aspect of the star.
Try these settings in the figure. ■

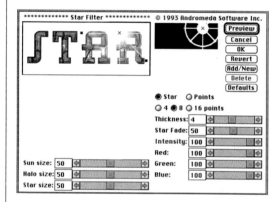

105

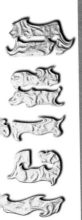

The Difference Clouds and Find Edges filters create this sticky texture and the Twirl filter pulls out the swirls to make this sweet effect.

1 Create a new file, and a new channel (#4). Use the Type Mask tool to enter the text. Any font will work with this effect, but I prefer something thick to give the filters enough room to work. I chose Impact at 100 points. You may want to add some spacing to make room for the swirls.

2 Choose Filter➔Render➔ Difference Clouds to start creating the texture.

3 The patterns in the clouds will become the swirling texture of the icing. To produce more variety, apply the Difference Clouds filter again. (I applied the filter four more times.) You can skip this step if you want.

TOOLBOX

Icing (Lighting
Style Preset)

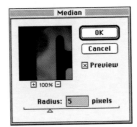

4 Next, choose Filter➔Noise➔ Median. The higher the Radius, the fewer the swirls that will appear inside the type. I set the Radius at 5. You will not, however, see the results of this filter until Step 6. The clouds should be little blurry now.

5 Choose Filter➡Stylize➡Find Edges.

6 Choose Image➡Adjust➡Invert. Now you should see faint white swirls—very faint.

7 Choose Image➡Adjust➡Levels. Slide the white (right) Input marker way over to the left. Then nudge the gray (middle) Input marker to the right—just a touch.

You want to get something like this:

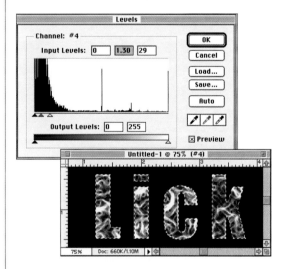

107

8 To get rid of the white border, choose Select➡Modify➡Contract. Contract the selection enough so that it no longer includes the white border. This selection is contracted 2 pixels.

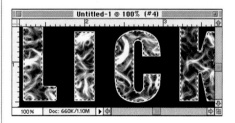

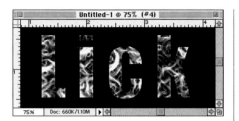

9 Choose Select➠Inverse, and press Delete to fill the selection with black.

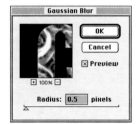

10 Choose Select➠Inverse. Now blur the swirls a little by choosing Filter➠Blur➠Gaussian Blur (Radius: 0.5). Deselect the text.

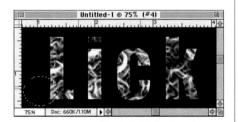

11 To get the swirls to extend past the hard edges, use the Twirl filter. First, select the Elliptical Marquee tool and make a selection like this.

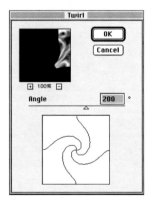

12 Then choose Filter➠Distort➠ Twirl. Watch the preview, and set the Angle so that a hook forms in the selection.

13 Keep making selections and applying the Twirl filter. I set the Twirl angle at 200, and pressed Command-F [Control-F] to reapply the Twirl filter with the same settings. To create more dramatic swirls, apply the filter to the same selection several times.

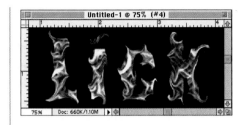

14 Double-click the Wand tool to select it and bring the Wand Options floating palette to the front. Set the Tolerance to 10, and click the Wand in a black area outside of the type. If you have letters with holes in them (such as o's and p's), then hold the Shift key down and click inside the holes as well. Choose Select➥ Inverse to select the swirled texture.

15 If your text has too much contrast (like mine), then choose Image➥Adjust➥Brightness➥ Contrast. Raise the Brightness (+40) and lower the Contrast (-30).

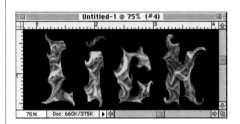

16 Finally, blur the text a little more by choosing Filter➥Blur➥ Gaussian Blur (Radius: 1).

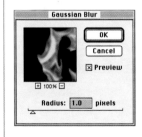

17 Return to the composite channel. The selection should still be active.

109

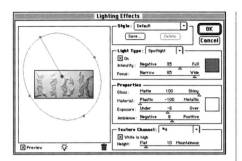

18 Choose Filter➛Render➛ Lighting Effects. Match the settings you see in this figure, or select the Icing preset from the pop-up menu. The Light Type color becomes the color of the icing. The CMYK values for this color are 35, 67, 5, 3.

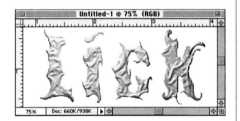

19 As a final touch I chose Select➛Modify➛Border (5 pixels) to select only the border. Then, I chose Filter➛Sharpen➛Sharpen Edges to harden the edges of the type.

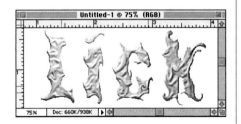

20 You can continue to do some swirling after you have applied the Lighting Effect filter, but your effect will look best if you keep the selection inside the type. ■

A little blurring and the Lighting Effects filter let you bang out this effect in no time.

1 Create a new file, and a new channel (#4). Use the Type tool to enter the text. Helvetica Condensed has that "license plate" look (70 points).

2 Deselect the text, and make a copy of this channel to create Channel #4 copy. Then choose Filter➡Blur➡Gaussian Blur (Radius: 3).

3 Load the selection Channel #4 copy (the same channel that is active).

4 Press Command-Option-F [Control-Option-F] to bring back the Gaussian Blur dialog box. Slide the Radius marker up until dark patches begin to appear at the ends of the letters. I set the Radius at 9 pixels for this example. Your text should look something like this.

112

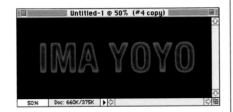

5 With the selection still active, press Command-I [Control-I] to invert the interior of the type.

6 Then choose Image➤Adjust➤ Brightness/Contrast and slide the Brightness marker up until your type looks something like what you see in the figure. Bring back almost all of the brightness. For me, this meant that I raised the Brightness all the way to +100, then chose Image➤Adjust➤ Brightness/Contrast again and raised the Brightness to +50.

7 Return to the composite channel. Load the original type selection (Channel #4). Choose Select➤Modify➤Contract (1 pixel), and Select➤Modify➤ Smooth (2 pixels), then Select➤Feather (1 pixel).

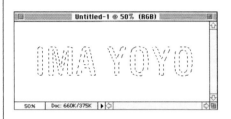

8 Change the foreground color to a color for the type. I used the CMYK values 0, 100, 100, 40. Fill the selection with the color.

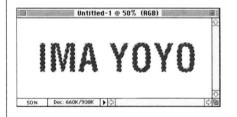

9 If you know license plates, then you probably have noticed how the ink is never quite centered on the raised metal. Deselect the type. Select the Move tool and use the arrow keys to move the type a little.

113

10 Choose Filter➤Render➤ Lighting Effects. Click on the Styles pop-up menu and select License Plate. If you have not loaded the presets from the CD, then match the settings as seen in this figure. ■

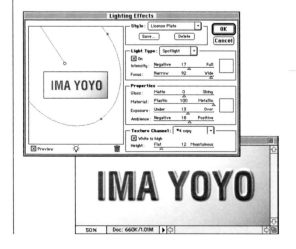

This simple effect creates lighted type that does not need a dark background. You also can create a snap with a variation of this technique.

1 Create a new file. Make a new layer (Layer 1), and change the foreground color to black.

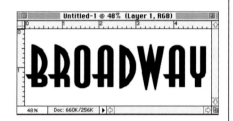

2 Next, use the Type tool to enter the text. This is Anna at 110 points.

3 Make another new layer (Layer 2), and load the transparency selection of Layer 1.

4 Choose Select➡Modify➡ Expand. Expand the selection so that you see a thin strip of white around the type. (I expanded this type selection 3 pixels.)

5 Hold the Command and Option [Control and Alt] keys and click the Layer 1 preview to subtract the transparency selection of Layer 1 from the current selection. You will see a minus sign appear inside of the box on the back of the hand pointer. The thin white strip created in Step 4 should now be selected.

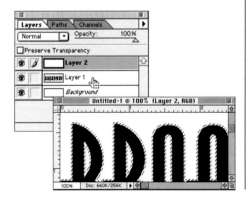

114

6 Fill the selection with 50% gray.

7 Create a new channel (#4), and fill the selection with white. Choose Filter➤Stylize➤Emboss and use these settings: Angle: 160°; Height: 1 pixel; Amount: 168%. Your settings may vary, but make sure that you see some contrast in the thin lines. The color should be a flat gray or white.

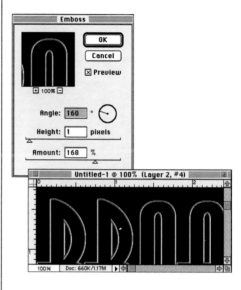

8 Return to the Composite channel. The selection should still be active, and Layer 2 should be the active layer.

115

9 Choose Filter➡Render➡Lighting Effects. Match these settings or select Outlines from the Styles pop-up menu.

10 Make a new layer (Layer 3), and load the transparency selection of Layer 1 (the original type selection).

11 Choose Select➡Feather. The amount that you feather the selection will depend on the point size of your type and the resolution of the file. You want to feather the selection enough so that it expands over the trim. (I feathered this type selection 5 pixels.)

12 Change the foreground color to a color for the light, and fill the selection to flip on the light switch. I used the CMYK values 0, 0, 94, 0.

VARIATIONS

You also can make each light a different color. After loading the Layer 1 transparency selection in Step 10, select the rectangular Marquee tool. Then hold down the Option and Shift [Alt and Shift] keys while dragging the Marque tool to create a selection around only the letter that you want, like this:

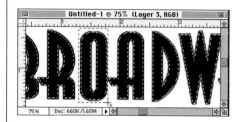

Proceed with Steps 11 and 12 to light up that letter.

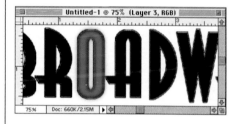

Repeat the process for each letter in the word.

You can always add the dark background by filling the background layer with black. I also loaded the Layer 1 transparency selection; I feathered (Select➝Feather) it 6 pixels, and filled it with white.

117

LIGHTS

This snap type was made using a similar technique that started with the Paintbrush tool.

1 Create a new file, and a new layer (Layer 1). Double-click the Paintbrush tool to select it and to bring forward the Paintbrush Options floating palette. Then click the Brushes tab to bring the Brushes palette to the front.

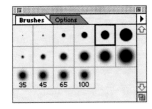

2 From the arrow menu on the Brushes palette, choose Reset Brushes to make sure that the default brushes are loaded. Click OK in the dialog box that opens.

3 Select any of the hard brushes, and change the Foreground color to black.

4 Use the brush and click one circle at a time to build your type.

TIP Turn on the Grid (View⇒ Show Grid) and the Snap to Grid (View⇒Snap to Grid) options to keep your circles in line.

5 Follow the instructions in Steps 3 through 12 starting on page 114. In Step 4, expand the selection only 2 pixels, and in Step 11, feather the selection 1 pixel.

6 Make the Background layer active, and load the transparency selection of Layer 2. Then load the transparency selection of Layer 3 while holding down the Shift key to add this selection to the existing selection. Choose Select➤ Feather (1 pixel), and fill the selection with black. Deselect the selection; select the Move tool, and nudge the selection to the right. ■

MARBLE

The Clouds filter helps create this realistic marble from scratch.

1 Create a new file. Use the Type Mask tool to enter the text. Marble looks good in a blocky font such as Machine (120 points).

2 Keep the selection active, and choose Filter➤Render➤Difference Clouds.

3 Reapply this filter a few times. The more times you apply the filter, the more the veins of the marble break up. I applied the Difference Clouds filter two times. Here is what my type looked like:

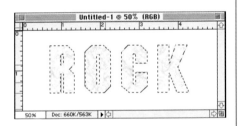

4 Choose Filter➤Stylize➤Find Edges. This filter pulls the veins out of the clouds.

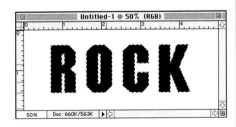

5 Choose Image➤Adjust➤Invert.

6 Next, choose Image➤Adjust➤ Levels. Grab the right (white) Input marker and slide it to the left until it sits under the beginning of the steep slope in the graph (shown in the figure). Then nudge the middle (gray) input marker to the right.

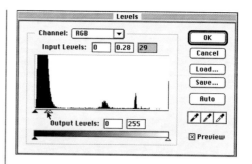

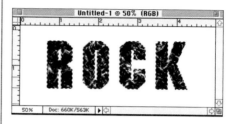

7 Choose Image➤Adjust➤ Hue/Saturation. Turn on the Colorize option. Then slide the Saturation marker down so that the color isn't too bright. I set the Saturation at 0. Use the Hue slider to find a color for the marble. For more color, nudge the Lightness up just a little.

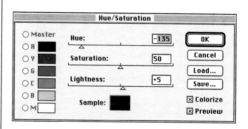

121

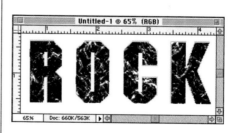

8 The Find Edges filter leaves a funny edge on the type. Choose Select➤Modify➤Contract. Contract the selection 1 or 2 pixels—just enough so that the selection is inside the marble. I chose 2 pixels. Choose Select➤Inverse and press Delete to fill the background with white. ■

Put your name in lights. The time-consuming part of this effect is building an even grid of lights; however, the new Guides and Grid feature in Adobe Photoshop 4.0 makes it a lot easier.

1 Create a new file. Change the foreground color to black (or another dark color) to contrast with the shining lights. Fill the Background layer with black.

2 Change the foreground color to white. Use the Type tool to enter the text. The type will drop automatically into a new layer (Layer 1). This type will serve as a guide for building the lights. Use a good fat font that can hold plenty of lights. I used City Bold at 60 points in this example. Move the type into place.

3 Use the Opacity slider on the Layers palette to lower the opacity of Layer 1 to 25%.

122

4 Make a new layer (Layer 2). Choose View➡Show Grid to turn on the grids.

5 Zoom in on the type so you can see one letter well. I zoomed in to 150%.

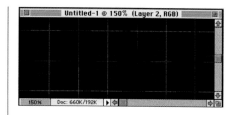

6 Choose File➔Preferences➔ Guides & Grid. The gridline distance determines how large the lights are relative to the type. As you change the Gridline distance setting, watch the image window to see how well the grid fits your type. Each grid square will become one light in your type. For this example, I set the Gridline every setting to 8 pixels, and kept the Subdivisions at 1.

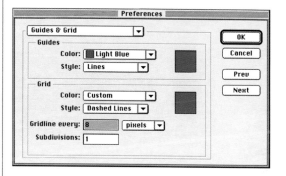

The image window is filled with lines.

7 Make Layer 1 the active layer and select the Move tool. Move the faded type into alignment with the grid. It does not have to be perfect since this type only serves as a guide for choosing where to place the lights. If it doesn't fit well, then change either the Grid or the type size.

8 Make Layer 2 the active layer again. Double-click the Marquee tool. Choose the Elliptical Marquee and set the style to fixed size. I set the fixed size to one-half the Gridline distance selected in Step 6. Make sure that you turn off Anti-Aliasing.

123

9 Also make sure that the View➛Snap to Guides option is turned on (it will have a check mark next to it). With the Marquee tool, click in the upper-left corner of the first grid box that you want to contain a light. The grid snap should align the fixed selection right into the corner.

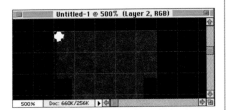

10 Fill the selection with white.

11 Keep clicking and filling, using the grid lines and the underlying type as guides. Here is the type after filling in all the lights.

12 Load the transparency selection of Layer 2. Then make a new layer (Layer 3), and make Layers 1 and 2 invisible.

13 Choose Select➛Feather (2 pixels) to soften the selection. Then fill the selection with white.

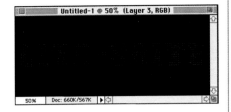

14 Change the foreground color to a color for the type. I used a bright yellow from Photoshop's default swatches.

15 Load the transparency selection of Layer 2 again. Choose Select➤ Feather. Feather the selection just 1 pixel this time. Fill it with the foreground color. ■

126

Mosaic (Lighting
Style Preset)

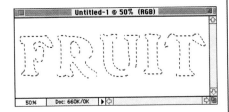

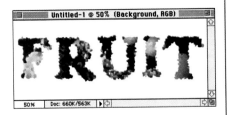

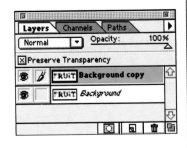

In this effect I will show you how to take an image and crack it into little pieces of color using the Crystallize filter.

1 Open a file that contains an image you can use for the mosaic tiles. Select the portion you want to use, copy it, and close the file. For this example I used the Fruit image from Photoshop's Tutorial file (Adobe Photoshop 4.0➡ Tutorial➡Fruit).

2 Create a new file, and use the Type Mask tool to enter the text. I used Frankenfont at 100 points. Keep the selection active.

3 Choose Edit➡Paste Into. The image you copied for your mosaic is pasted into the selected text. Choose Layer➡Merge Down to bring everything back to the Background layer.

4 Choose Filter➡Pixelate➡ Crystallize, and type in a Cell (tile) Size (10).

5 It's a good start, but we need some grout. Make a copy of this layer to create the Background layer copy.

6 To create the lines for the grout, choose Filter➔Stylize➔Find Edges.

7 To clean up the lines do the following commands: Image➔Adjust➔Threshold (255), and Filter➔Other➔Maximum (Radius: 1). Your image should transform like this:

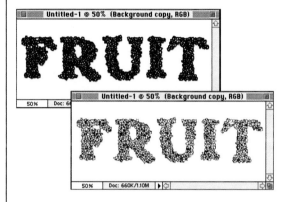

8 Select the Magic Wand tool and be very careful to click on a white area inside your text in the Background layer copy. Then choose Select➔Similar. All the white in this layer will be selected. Press Delete, and deselect the selection. Presto, mosaic type.

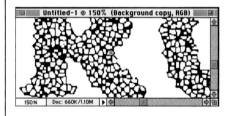

127

TIP If the selection was filled rather than deleted when you pressed Delete in Step 8, then undo the action, turn off the Preserve Transparency option on the Layers palette, and try it again.

Mosaic

VARIATIONS

This method is similar to the previous one; however, a few extra steps will improve the appearance of the grout.

1 Perform Step 1. (For this variation, I used the same image that was used in the previous steps.)

2 Then create a new channel (#4), and use the Type tool to enter the text. (Again, I used Frankenfont at 100 points.) Deselect the text.

3 Choose Filter➤Pixelate➤Crystallize (Cell Size: 10), and Image➤Adjust➤Threshold (255).

4 Return to the composite channel, load the selection Channel #4, and choose Edit➤Paste Into. Choose Layer➤Merge Down to bring everything back to the Background layer.

5 Break up the image again by choosing Filter➤Pixelate➤Crystallize (Cell Size: 10).

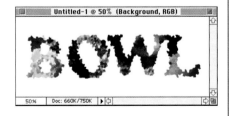

6 Select the entire image, and copy it. Then create a new channel, and paste in the image. Deselect the selection.

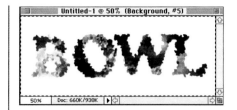

7 Now, complete Steps 6 and 7. Then press Command-I [Control-I] to invert the channel. Here is what I have now.

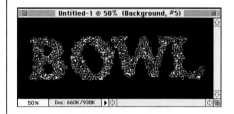

8 Duplicate this channel to create Channel #5 copy.

9 Choose Filter➡Blur➡Gaussian Blur (Radius: 1 pixel).

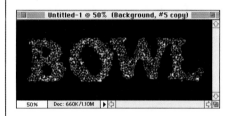

10 Now we are ready to finish it. Return to the composite channel, load the selection Channel #5, and fill it with white.

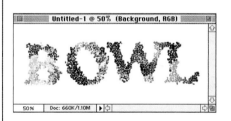

129

11 Keep the selection active, and choose Filter➡Render➡Lighting Effects. Then select the Mosaic preset from the Style pop-up menu, or match the settings you see here. Make sure that Channel #5 copy is the texture channel.

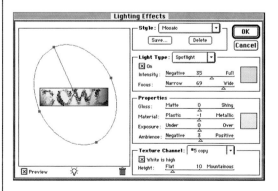

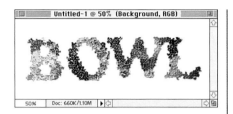

`Untitled-1 @ 50%  (Background, RGB)`

`50%` `Doc: 660K/1.10M`

12 Beautiful mosaic type.

13 If you turn off the White is High checkbox in the Lighting Effects filter dialog box, then you will get this. ■

The Tiles filter breaks up type into a grid. Then some texture is added with the Wind filter. Finally, the Lighting Effects filter brings everything together.

1 Create a new file. I created an oversized file (5" wide x 3" tall) because in Step 7 we will need room to rotate the text. Create a new channel (#4), and use the Type tool to enter the text. This is another effect that needs a thick, hefty font. Poplar at 120 points was used for this example.

2 Choose Filter➔Stylize➔Tiles. This filter does most of the work by establishing the grid. Find a Number of Tiles that looks good in the type. I used 10. Keep the Offset percentage set at 1.

3 Choose Image➔Adjust➔Invert.

TOOLBOX

Net (Lighting Style Preset)

4 If you hide the selection edges (Command-H) [Control-H], you can see that there are thin lines on some of the edges of the corners. To get rid of them, choose Select➤Modify➤Contract (1 pixel), and Select➤Inverse. Next fill the selection with black.

 To get rid of any leftover strange edges, choose Select➤Inverse again. Then set the foreground color to black and use the paintbrush to paint away the edges. If you choose Select➤Inverse to perform this Tip, then skip that part of the next step.

5 Choose Select➤Inverse again. Then choose Filter➤Other➤ Maximum (Radius: 1). This thickens the lines of the grid. These lines become the ropes in the net: the thicker the lines, the thicker the ropes.

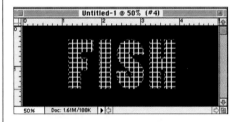

6 Then, choose Filter➤Noise➤ Median (Radius: 1 or 2) to round out the intersections. Deselect the grid.

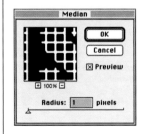

133

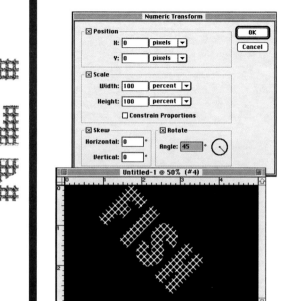

7 Now for the texture. First, make sure that the background color is black. Then, rotate the entire image 45° by choosing Layer➤ Transform➤Numeric (Angle: 45°). After the image rotates, make sure that all of the type is still visible.

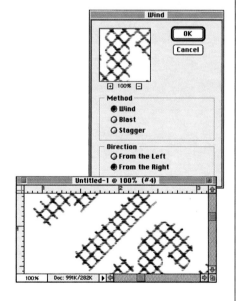

8 Invert the entire image (Command-I) [Control-I]. Next, apply the Wind filter twice. Once to the left and once to the right by choosing Filter➤Stylize➤Wind (Wind, Left) and Filter➤Stylize➤ Wind (Wind, Right).

9 Invert the image again (Command-I) [Control-I]. Then rotate it back to its horizontal position by choosing Layer➤ Transform➤Numeric (Angle: -45°).

10 Return to the composite channel. Load the selection Channel #4. Choose Filter➤Render➤ Lighting Effects and select Net from the Style pop-up menu or match the settings seen here. Make sure that Channel #4 is selected as the texture channel. The color of the light will become the color of the net.

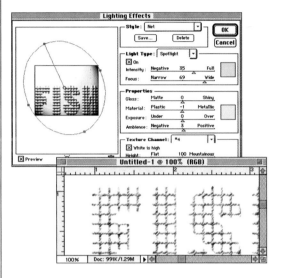

11 For this example, the Lighting Effects filter was applied a second time by pressing Command-F [Control-F].

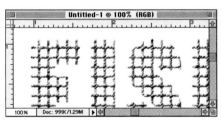

135

12 And finally everything was made a little darker using the Levels dialog box.

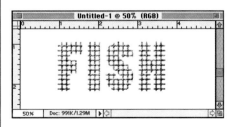

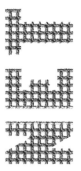

A Rougher Rope

1 Perform Steps 1 through 6 previously listed. Then choose Filter➤ Stylize➤Diffuse (Normal).

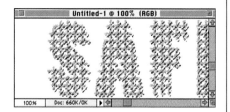

2 Return to the composite channel, and load the selection Channel #4. Choose a foreground color and fill the selection. I used these CMYK values: 17, 24, 74, 4.

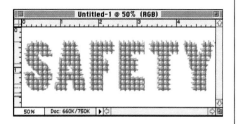

3 Now, select the Marquee tool and press the down arrow and right arrow keys three times each to move the selection.

4 Choose another foreground color (I used these CMYK values: 30, 55, 100, 42), and fill the selection.

5 Again, with the Marquee tool selected, press the up arrow and left arrow keys two times each. Then, select the Move tool and press the up arrow and left arrow keys one time each. ■

Creating this effect is very similar to creating the Foil effect. Try the subtle changes offered in the Variations section. They improve the look of the paper quite a bit.

1 Create a new file. It must be an RGB file so that you can use the Lighting Effects filter. Create a new channel (#4).

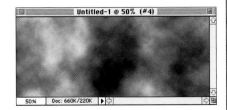

2 To start creating the paper texture, choose Filter➤Render➤ Clouds. Channel #4 should look like this.

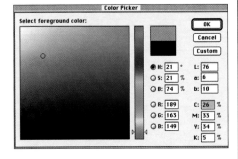

3 Now go back to the Composite channel (Command-~) [Control-~] and choose a brown paper color for the foreground color. The CMYK values 26, 33, 34, 5 worked well for this effect.

4 Use the Type Mask tool to enter the text. BadgerBold at 70 points was used for this example. Move the type selection into place, and then fill it with the foreground color. Do not deselect the text.

TOOLBOX

Brown Paper Bag
(Lighting Style
Preset)

5 So, we've got brown—but we need paper. Choose Filter➤ Render➤Lighting Effects and choose BrownPaperBag from the Style menu, or match the settings as seen in this figure.

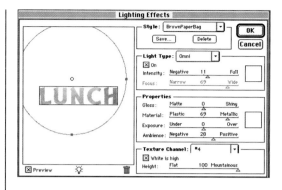

6 Click OK, deselect the selection, and you are ready for lunch.

VARIATIONS

Giving the letters rough edges adds to the paper effect. After entering the text in Step 4, press Q to switch to the Quick Mask mode. Next, choose Filter➤ Pixellate➤Crystallize (Cell Size: 5). Then choose Image➤Adjust➤ Threshold (Level: 9). Press Q again to exit the Quick Mask mode. Finish Step 4 and the remainder of the steps. I also chose Image➤Adjust➤ Brightness/Contrast and increased the contrast to +40 for this varia-tion. Finally, add a shadow to give the effect of floating paper letters.

139

LUNCH

Darker edges can help define the paper's edges. With the type still selected—after applying the Lighting Effects filter in Step 5—save the selection. Next choose Select➤Modify➤Border. Use a Width appropriate for your type. I chose 5 pixels. Then choose Image➤Adjust➤Brightness/Contrast (Brightness: -31; Contrast: 25). You can get rid of the fuzz created around the letters by loading the type selection you just saved, and choosing Select➤Inverse to invert the selection. Hit Delete to fill the selection with white. ■

142

Here's a quick and easy one that takes advantage of one of Photoshop's distort filters. You guessed it: Pinch.

1 Create a new file. Choose a color for the type and use the Type tool to enter the text (Palatino Bold, 90 points). Choose Layer➤Merge Down to put the type back on the Background layer.

2 The key to getting the most from your pinches is the selection you make. Use the rectangular Marquee tool and drag a rectangle around the first letter, like this.

3 Next, choose Filter➤Distort➤ Pinch (Amount: 100). Play with the slider and watch the effect on the preview. Click OK and you should see something like this.

4 Repeat Steps 2 and 3 for all the letters in the word. Experiment with the selections you make. Here are the selections I made for the rest of the letters.

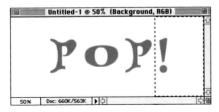

Remember you can use **Command-Option-F (Control-Alt-F)** to recall the dialog box from the last filter used. So, make your selection, press **Command-Option-F**, slide, and click **OK**.

5 And here's what you get.

6 But you don't have to stop there. After pinching the individual letters, I selected the entire image and pinched it.

7 Then select just the "O", and choose Filter➡Distort➡Twirl (Amount: 999%). Keep experimenting.

VARIATIONS

For this variation, I selected a rectangle around half of the text at a time. With the left half selected, I chose Layer➡Transform➡ Perspective to distort the text. Then I used the Pinch filter (Filter➡Distort➡Pinch) with a positive setting. I treated the right half of the text the same, except I used a negative setting in the Pinch filter dialog box. ■

Plaid

TOOLBOX

Plaid (Lighting
Style Preset)

This effect works by combining four Photoshop filters (Fragment, Mosaic, Tile, and Facet) that can be used in various combinations to make different plaids. I found that the following method works the best.

1 First, create a new file. Choose a foreground color for the color of the type, then use the Type Mask tool to enter the text into a layer. I used 90 point Berliner-Plain type. Fill it with the foreground color.

2 Keep the selection active and choose Filter➞Stylize➞Tile (Number of Tiles: 10; Maximum Offset: 1%). The Number of Tiles controls the number of vertical tiles that will be in your tallest letter. You can change the number of tiles, but keep the maximum offset at 1% so the grid's lines are straight.

3 Now, go to the Channels palette and click on one of the color channels to make it the only active channel. (I made the Red channel the active channel). The tiled type looks gray, since you are only viewing one color channel.

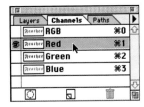

By choosing a different color channel in Step 3, you will see different colors when you return to the composite channel in Step 5. You can also make two color channels active.

4 Choose Filter➤Pixellate➤ Fragment. There are no settings for this filter; the type will divide into even smaller segments.

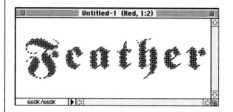

5 Now, for the magic. Press Command-~ [Control-~] to return to the composite channel. Instant plaid waiting for you. Using the Fragment filter to shift the pixels of only one color channel produces new segments and colors.

6 To change the colors of the plaid, choose Image➤Adjust➤ Hue/Saturation and use the Hue slider to run through a closet full of plaids.

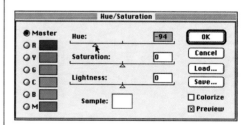

145

7 Here's the final type.

VARIATIONS

The possibilities are endless. Here is a selection of plaids I made by applying just one more filter to the previous above:

Select the Red channel and choose Filter➤Other➤Maximum (Radius: 2).

Or, try choosing Filter➤Pixellate➤Fragment. Keep applying the filter until the plaid glows.

Try Filter➤Pixelate➤Facet, and reapply the filter (Command-F) [Control-F] a few times.

Filter➤Stylize➤Find Edges applied several times.

Or, choose only one color channel. (I chose the Green channel.) Choose Filter➤Stylize➤Find Edges, and apply the filter a second time (Command-F) [Control-F].

Add Some Texture

Keep the type selection active and choose Filter➤Render➤Lighting Effects. Use the settings shown here, or choose the Plaid preset from the Style pop-up menu. The most important setting is the texture channel. Choose one of the RGB channels. After you hit OK, the plaid will look like it has some texture.

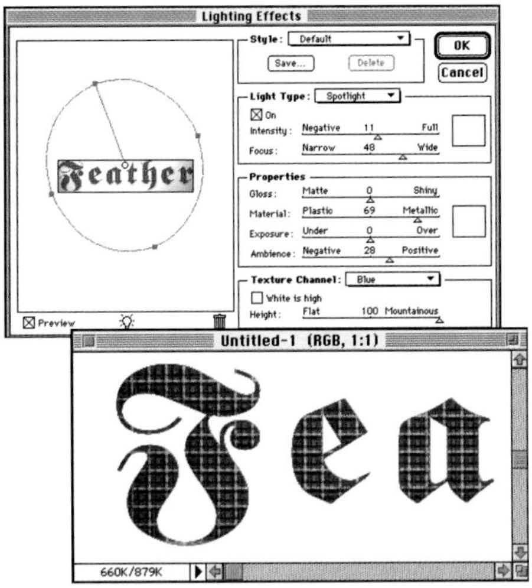

146

Monochrome Plaid

For a monochrome plaid with thick and thin cross lines, complete Steps 1 and 2; then choose Filter➡Pixellate➡Mosaic. Watch the preview to find a Cell Size that gives you the desired effect. A Cell Size of 4 worked for me.

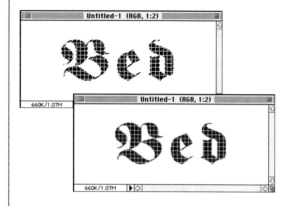

One More Road to Plaid

Complete Steps 1 through 3. Then, choose Filter➡Pixellate➡Mosaic (Cell Size: 6). ■

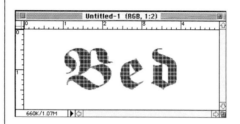

To set up the diamond pattern, this effect borrows a few steps from the Checkered effect (page 44), and then color is added at the end.

1 Create a new file. Double-click the Marquee tool to select it and bring the Marquee Options floating palette to the front. Change the Style to Fixed Size. The values you enter for the Width and Height determine the size of the diamonds. It is important that you use the same values for both. I used 7.

2 Zoom in to an area of the blank image and click with the Marquee tool to make a square selection. Fill the selection with black.

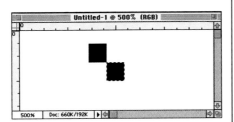

3 Then move the selection to line up opposite corners of the selection and the black square. Fill the selection.

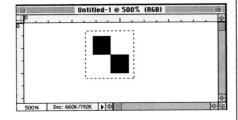

4 Next, change the Marquee tool Style to Normal, and make a selection that encompasses both of the black squares.

5 Choose Layer➔Transform➔ Numeric, and turn off all the options except for the Rotate option. Set the Rotate value at 45°. Deselect the selection. You should have something like this:

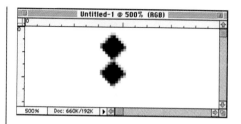

6 Change the Marquee tool Style to Constrain Aspect Ratio. Leave the Width and Height values at 1. Then click and drag a selection like this:

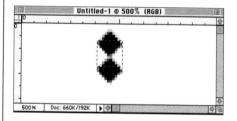

7 Choose Edit➔Define Pattern to save the selection as a pattern.

8 Then choose Select➔All and Edit➔Fill. Change the Contents option to Pattern. Here is the full image area:

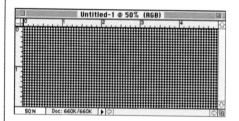

9 Use the Type Mask tool to enter the text. I used East Bloc at 100 points, a font big enough to show off the effect.

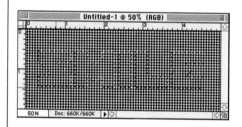

149

10 Choose Select➔Inverse, and press Delete.

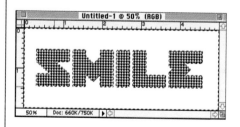

11 Choose Select➤Inverse again. Make a new layer (Layer 1).

12 Double-click the Gradient tool to select it and bring to the front the Gradient Options floating palette. Choose the Spectrum preset gradient, and set the Type to Linear.

13 Drag the Gradient tool diagonally across the type selection, like this:

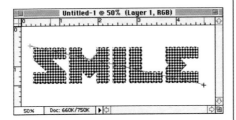

The selection will fill with the gradient.

14 Change the Layer 1 blending mode to Color. The diamonds reappear.

15 Keep the selection active and make the Background layer the active layer.

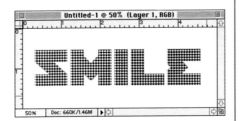

16 Choose Filter➤Render➤ Difference Clouds to complete the effect.

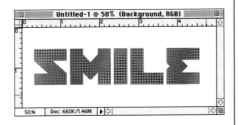

VARIATIONS

After Step 16, you can reapply the Difference Clouds filter as many times as you like to create more variation in the values of the diamonds. Choose the foreground color before you apply the filter and watch the different effects. If the image gets too dark or has too much contrast, then use the Hue/Saturation dialog box to adjust the values of Layer 1 (Image➔Adjust➔Hue/Saturation).

Or, you can choose Image➔ Adjust➔Brightness/Contrast and raise the Contrast (+78) and Brightness (+48) sliders.

Or, you can apply Filter➔Noise➔ Add Noise (Amount: 80).

Or, you can choose Filter➔ Stylize➔Find Edges.

For this one, keep the type selection active, and make a new layer (Layer 2). Then open the Flower file from Photoshop's Tutorial files and choose Edit➔Paste Into to paste it into the text selection. Then, change the Layer 2 blending mode to Difference. I also added a 3-pixel black stroke. ■

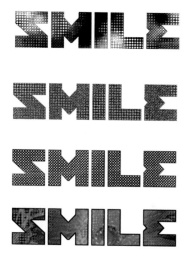

151

Rip it up and put it back together again. After letting the Crystallize and Glowing Edges filters tear up the type, the Wand tool will come in handy for scattering them around the image.

1 Create a new file. Change the foreground color to black. Use the Type tool to enter the text. (I used Playbill at 90 points.) The text will be automatically placed in a new layer (Layer 1).

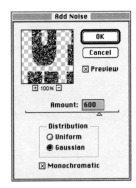

2 Choose Filter➔Noise➔Add Noise. Set the amount to about 600, and check the Monochromatic box.

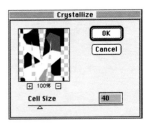

3 Filter➔Pixelate➔Crystallize. Use a large Cell Size relative to your type. I chose 40.

Your type should look something like this now.

152

TIP You can see how the type is split into pieces. If you don't like how the pieces are arranged, then press Command-Z [Control-Z] to undo the filter, and Command-F [Control-F] to redo the filter. The pieces will be randomly redistributed.

4 Choose Filter➤Stylize➤Glowing Edges. This new Photoshop 4.0 filter saves a couple of steps. Use these settings: Edge Width: 1, Edge Brightness: 20, and Smoothness: 1.

Now the type should be split into pieces.

5 Choose Select➤Color Range. Using the left eyedropper tool in the dialog box, click one of the pieces of your type. Set the Fuzziness to 200, and turn on the Invert option.

153

Everything but pieces should be selected. The selection should look like this.

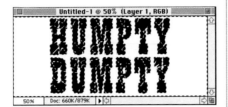

6 Make sure that the Preserve Transparency is turned off. Press Delete. Not much will change, but the white lines between the black pieces are now gone.

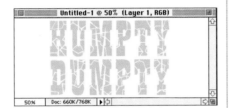

7 Deselect the pieces, and turn on Preserve Transparency for Layer 1. Choose a foreground color for the type, and fill the selection with the color.

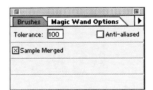

8 Double-click the Wand tool to select it and bring the Magic Wand Options floating palette to the front. Change the tolerance to 100, and turn on the Sample Merged option.

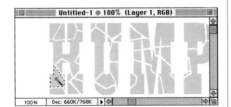

Using the Wand tool, click on one of the colored pieces to select it. Then follow Step 9 to move the colored piece. Next, select another piece with the Wand tool, and then do Step 9 again, and so on....Continue doing this until all the pieces are properly scattered.

154

9 Select the Move tool. You can now use the arrow keys or the mouse to shift the pieces. Also try using the Rotate feature (Layer➤Transform➤Rotate) on some of the pieces. Generally, I moved the pieces closer to each other, and tried to make their placement look more scattered. You might also try deleting some of the tinier pieces.

10 Load the transparency selection of Layer 1 to select all of the pieces.

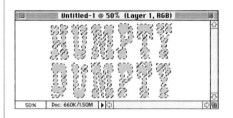

11 Make a new layer (Layer 2) and move it below Layer 1.

12 Choose Select➤Feather, and feather the selection a small amount. I chose 1 pixel.

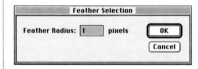

155

13 Layer 2 is for the shadow. However, I want the scrap pieces to look like they are floating a little. Press Q to enter Quick Mask mode. The area around the selection will probably turn red (unless you have changed the default settings).

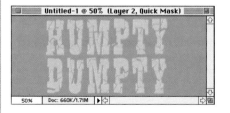

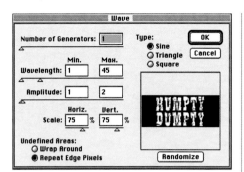

14 Choose Filter➤Distort➤Wave. Use the settings shown in this figure (Number: 1, Wavelength: 1/45, Amplitude: 1/2, Horizontal Scale: 75%, Vertical Scale: 75%, Type: Sine, Undefined Areas: Repeat edge pixels). You are actually waving the selection, not the type.

The image window will not look much different. There should be a few white specks around the edges of the letters.

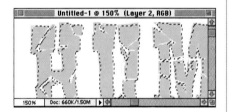

15 Press Q to exit Quick Mask mode. To shift the shadow, select the Marquee tool. Move the selection one keystroke to the right and one keystroke down.

16 Change the foreground color to black (or another color for the shadow), fill the selection, and you're finished.

VARIATION

To add some curvature to the pieces, choose Filter➤Distort➤ Wave before Step 10. Use the same settings as in Step 14. This step puts just a little bend in the pieces.

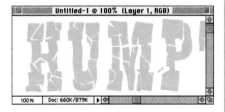

The finished type should look like this. ■

TOOLBOX

Spaghetti
(Lighting Style
Preset)

The Noise and Crystallize filters set up the Find Edges filter to create this quick effect. You will have plenty of time to check out the variations.

1 Create a new file. Set the foreground color to black and the background color to white (press D). Use the Type Mask tool to enter the text. For this example, I used 100-point Gadzoox. Move the text selection into place, and fill it with black.

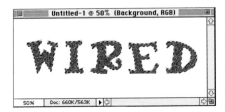

2 Choose Filter➡Noise➡Add Noise (Gaussian, do not turn on Monochromatic). Slide the marker to the right—to about 600.

3 Copy the noisy type, create a new channel (#4), and paste in the noise, which will now be gray. (Channels cannot show color.) Deselect the text.

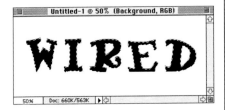

4 Choose Filter➡Pixelate➡ Crystallize. The Cell Size here is going to determine the density of the scribbles. I chose a cell size of 8. You can look ahead to Step 7 to see how the scribbles turned out.

5 Now, choose Filter➥Stylize➥ Find Edges. The scribbling begins.

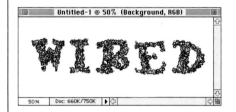

6 Invert the channel (Command-I) [Control-I]. Return to the Composite channel. Select the entire image (Command-A) [Control-A] and press Delete to clear the image area.

7 The foreground color should still be black. Load the selection Channel #4, and fill it with black.

VARIATIONS

I had a lot of fun with this one. There are many simple things you can do with this technique.

If you perform Steps 1 and 2, skip Step 3, deselect the text, use a Cell Size of 5 in Step 4, and stop after Step 5, you get this effect:

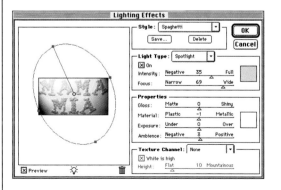

159

Spaghetti, anyone? Perform all the previous steps except Step 7. Then go to the Channels palette and duplicate Channel #4 to create Channel #4 copy. Choose Filter➥Blur➥Gaussian Blur (Radius: .5). Return to the Composite channel and load the selection Channel #4. Choose Select➥ Modify➥Expand (1 pixel). Change the foreground color to the CMYK

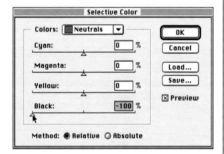

values: 0, 12, 15, 25. Fill the selection. Apply Filter➟Render➟ Lighting Effects. Click on the Style pop-up menu and find the Spaghetti preset, or match the settings seen on the previous page. Make sure Channel #4 copy is the texture channel. Finally, to thin down the spaghetti, choose Select➟Inverse and press Delete to fill the selection with white.

Perform Steps 1 and 2. Skip Step 3. Deselect the text. Use a Cell Size of 5 in Step 4 and do Step 5 as described. Then choose Image➟Adjust➟Hue/Saturation and type -100 in the Saturation box. Next choose Image➟Adjust➟ Selective Color. Choose Neutrals from the pop-up menu and slide the black marker all the way to the left (-100%). Do the same for the Whites. You should get this effect.

OK, so I have strayed a little from scribbling. Why stop now? Do Steps 1 and 2. Deselect the text. Choose Filter➟Noise➟Median (Radius: 5). ■

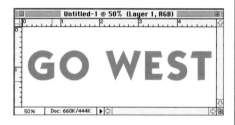

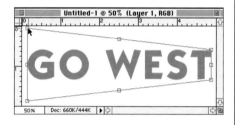

TOOLBOX

KPT Planar
Tiling Filter

Photoshop does not have true 3D capabilities, but you can perform a few tricks with the Transform feature that will make your type look like it is sitting on a 3D surface.

1 Create a new file, and use the Type tool to enter the text. This font is Kabel at 75 points. The type will be placed automatically into a new layer.

The Simple Receding Surface

Method 1. Choose Layer➛ Transform➛Perspective. Grab a corner point and drag it toward one of its adjacent corners. The type pinches to look like it recedes. You also can drag in the opposite direction to stretch the text at one end. When finished, press the Return [Enter] key to accept the changes, or Command-. [Control-.] to cancel the changes. It may take you a few minutes to get used to the way the box reacts when you drag one of the corners, but it's really pretty simple.

TIP The Undo command still works while you are distorting the type; it will undo only the last distortion, however.

Method 2. Choose Layer➡Free Transform. The transform feature can distort the text in many ways. The advantage to using this feature is that you can change the size of the type at the same time that you pinch or stretch it. To activate the Perspective feature while using the Free Transform feature, hold the Command, Option, and Shift [Control, Alt, and Shift] keys while dragging a corner. To change the size of the type, click and drag on one of the side points.

TIP All of the Effects tools work the same way. To make a change, click one of the corner tabs and drag it. You can continue to alter the text in this manner. Then, when you are finished, press Return [Enter] to accept the changes. To cancel the changes, press Command-. [Control-.].

3 What if you want to put type across the bend of two walls? Use the Perspective feature as you did above, but select only the part of the text that will be on the receding surface.

All of these samples were created with the Perspective feature using one of the previous methods.

4 And, what if you want to put the text on a receding corner? This effect is a bit more complicated, but it is still just a matter of making the proper selection and using the Transform tools. It is the order in which you do these tasks that makes the difference.

5 First (in a new file) draw a simple line with the Line tool. Just choose a foreground color for the lines, select the Line tool and click and drag.

6 Do Step 1, except use the Type Mask tool instead of the Type tool. Then save the text selection to create Channel #4.

7 Use the rectangular Marquee tool to select the top half of the type.

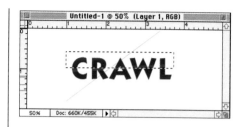

8 Choose Layer➤Transform➤ Skew. Hold the Option [Alt] key and drag one of the top points to the left—about as far as shown in the figure (approximately 45°). Then press the Return [Enter] key, and deselect the text.

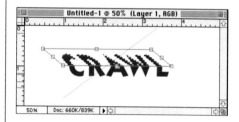

9 Select the bottom half of the text.

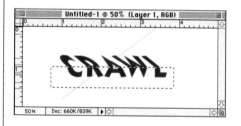

10 Choose Layer➤Transform➤ Skew again, and pull the box back the same distance.

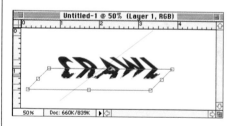

165

The type should look like this now.

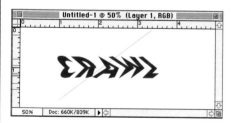

11 Deselect the text, and choose Layer➤Free Transform. Click on the top-right corner point, hold the Command, Option, and Shift [Control, Alt, and Shift] keys, and drag it down about one fourth of the height of the text.

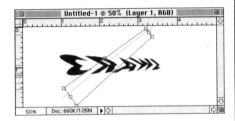

12 Now move the pointer outside of the distortion box. It will turn into a corner icon with two arrows. Click and drag to rotate the text.

13 Move the pointer inside the text box until it turns into a solid black arrow. Click and drag to move the type into place over the receding line.

14 Press the Return [Enter] key to accept the changes.

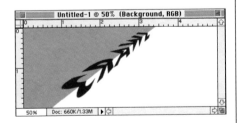

15 I drew a darker plane to represent the top surface of the receding corner.

Other Surfaces

On page 20, you can find out
how to put type on a ball.

KPT Planar Tiling

KPT 3.0 contains a filter that will
tile your text onto a receding
plane. Use the Type tool to enter
the text. Choose Layer➡
Transform➡Scale and stretch the
text until it fills the image window.

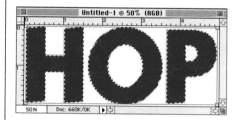

Deselect the text. Choose
Filter➡KPT 3.0➡KPT Planar Tiling
3.0. From the Mode menu choose
Perspective tiling. Then click on
the preview and drag the pointer
around. The Height and Shear will
adjust as you drag. When you find
the desired effect, click the green
button. ■

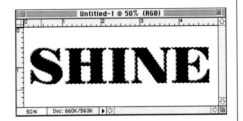

A simple effect brought to you by the under-used Maximum filter. This filter spreads the white areas of the type into shimmering blocks of light.

1 Create a new file. Use the Type Mask tool to enter the text. Century Black at 90 points was used for this example. Fill the text with black.

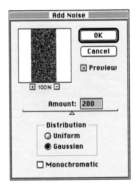

2 To break up the text, add some noise by choosing Filter➥Noise➥ Add Noise. I set the Amount to 200.

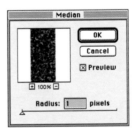

3 Then choose Filter➥Noise➥ Median. Try different settings, but keep it low. I used the minimum: 1 pixel. Deselect the text.

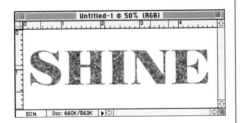

4 Choose Filter➥Other➥ Maximum. Again, use a low setting. I used a Radius of 2.

168

VARIATIONS

Variations abound for this simple effect.

For brighter text, try the following settings in Steps 2 through 4: Noise: 500; Median: 2; Maximum: 2.

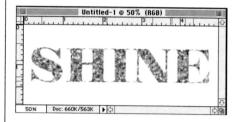

To narrow the color range, fill the text with a color other than black in Step 1. The CMYK values for the color I used are: 0, 72, 72, 0.

In Step 2, set the Noise amount low. I used 50.

Do Steps 3 and 4 as described.

169

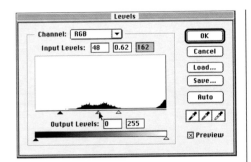

Since the color is a little on the pale side, choose Image➟ Adjust➟Levels. Move the black and the white sliders closer to the center.

After Step 4, try applying Filter➟Stylize➟Find Edges to turn the colored areas into colored lines.

Adding more white to the type will make it look more like its shining. Choose Filter➟Other➟ Maximum (Radius: 1).

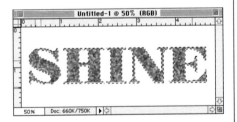

In Step 3, save the selection (to create Channel #4) before deselecting the text. Then after Step 4, load the selection Channel #4.

Copy the shimmering text and create a new channel (Channel #5). The selection should still be active. Paste in the type, which will now be black-and-white.

Choose Image➡Adjust➡Levels, and slide the middle (gray) marker to the left until the Input Level box reads 0.25. The channel should look like this:

Return to the composite channel, and make a new layer (Layer 1). Then load the selection Channel #5.

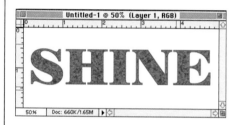

Change the foreground color to a color for the text. I used the CMYK values: 100, 75, 0, 0. Fill the selection.

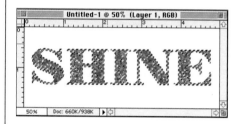

Now, play around with the layer mode settings for unique effects. For this image I chose Dissolve, and set the Layer 1 Opacity at 80%. ■

171

1 If you want an image to show through the glass type, then open it now. Otherwise, create a new file.

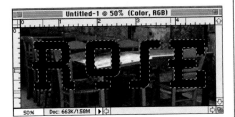

2 Make a new layer and name it Color. Change the foreground color to black (press D), and use the Type Mask tool to enter the text. A heavy typeface will give you plenty of room to divide the letters into smaller sections of glass. This font is Knomen at 180 points. Fill the text with black. Save the type selection to create Channel #4.

3 Back in the Color layer, choose Filter➔Noise➔Add Noise (Amount: 560). The Noise filter breaks up the type and adds the color to the glass.

Add Noise

OK

Cancel

☒ Preview

⊞ 100% ⊟

Amount: 560

Distribution
○ Uniform
● Gaussian

☐ Monochromatic

172

TOOLBOX

Glass (Lighting Style Preset)

Trim (Lighting Style Preset)

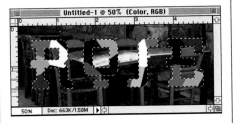

4 Then choose Filter➔Pixelate➔ Crystallize. This filter establishes the shapes of the glass divisions. Watch the preview, and choose a Cell Size that is right for your text. I chose 100.

5 Choose Layer➥New➥Layer Via Copy. A new layer is created. Change its name to Trim.

6 Choose Filter➥Stylize➥Find Edges, and then Image➥Adjust➥ Threshold (255). You can now see the beginnings of the trim.

7 Select the Magic Wand tool, and set the tolerance in its floating palette to 1. Click the wand in a white area of the type.

Then choose Select➥Similar.

173

8 Press Delete to leave only the black lines in the Trim layer. You will see the colors in the Color layer pop through.

9 Save the active selection to create Channel #5, and then make Channel #5 the active channel. Deselect the selection.

10 Make a copy of this channel to create Channel #5 copy. While in Channel #5 copy, choose Filter➟ Blur➟Gaussian Blur (Radius: 2.5).

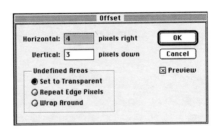

11 Make a copy of this channel to create Channel #5 copy 2. Take a look at the Channels palette in the figure and make sure that you have all of these channels.

12 Then choose Filter➟ Other➟Offset (Horizontal: -4; Vertical: -3).

174

13 Choose Image➔Calculations. Here is the dialog box you will see. Match the settings on your screen to the ones you see here.

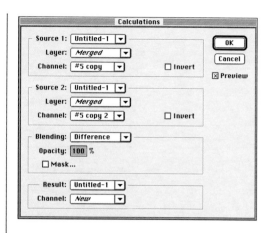

A new channel (#8) is created that should look like this.

14 Press Command-I [Control-I] to invert the channel, and then choose Image➔Adjust➔Auto Levels. The contrast in this channel will increase.

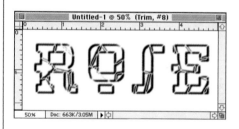

175

15 Okay, back to the layers. Return to the composite channel. Everything here is still the same.

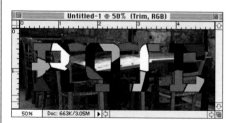

16 Make the Background layer the active layer and the only visible layer.

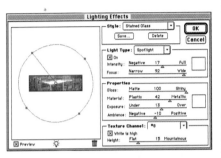

17 Load the selection Channel #5, and choose Filter➞Render➞ Lighting Effects. Match your settings to this dialog box, or choose Glass from the pop-up Style menu. Change the Texture channel to Channel #8.

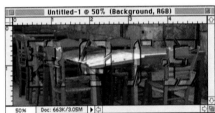

176

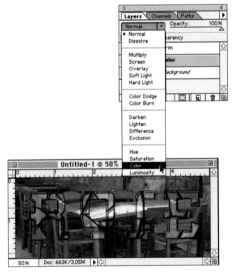

18 Now, make all of the layers visible and make the Color layer the active layer. Change the mode of the Color layer to Color. That's our stained glass. Now, let's fix the trim.

19 Make the Trim layer the active layer and load the selection Channel #4 (the original text outlines). Choose Edit➔Stroke. Match the settings here.

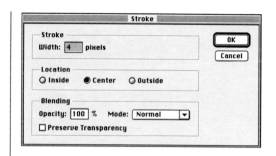

20 Load the selection of the Trim Layer Transparency to select the trim lines. Change foreground color to a color for the trim. I just used 50% gray. Fill the selection.

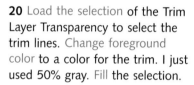

21 Save the selection to create Channel #9. Make Channel #9 the active channel, and choose Filter➔Stylize➔Emboss (Angle: 144, Height: 3, and Amount: 125%). This channel will help the Lighting Effects filter—in the next step—add some dimension to the trim between the colored panes.

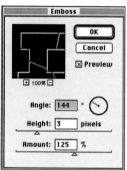

22 Return to the composite channel and the Trim layer. The selection should still be active. Choose Filter➔Render➔Lighting Effects. Choose Trim from the Style pop-up menu, or match these settings.

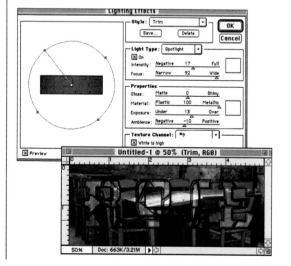

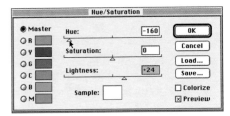

23 Now, that's better. However, what if you still don't like the colors? Follow me. Make the Color layer the active layer. Select the Magic Wand tool and click on any glass pane.

24 You now can use any of Photoshop's color adjusting features to change the color of this pane. The simplest way is to choose Image➛Adjust➛Hue/Saturation. Use the sliders to find a color.

> **TIP** You almost always will have a couple of black glass panes that you will want to change. This happens because the Noise filter you applied earlier in Step 3 includes some black.

25 Keep repeating Steps 23 and 24 until all the colors meet your demanding standards.

VARIATIONS

If you want to get rid of the background, then follow these steps. Flatten the image. Load the selection Channel #4 (the original text selection). Choose Select➛Modify➛Expand (1 pixel). Choose Select➛Inverse. Change the background color to white, and then press Delete. ∎

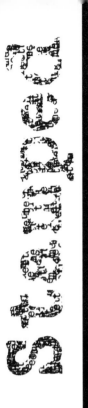

This technique shows you how to make type stamps that you can use to build words or patterns.

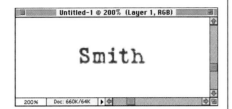

1 Create a new file. Use the Type tool to enter the text. Use a small point size. The type that was used here is Love Letter Typewriter at 10 points. Press Command-E [Control-E] to merge the new layer created by the Type tool back into the Background.

TIP When using small point sizes, you may prefer to turn off the anti-aliasing option in the Type dialog box. If you don't, then the type may be blurred.

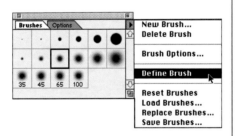

2 Zoom in on the type. Then select the Marquee tool and drag a rectangular selection around the type.

3 Double-click the Paintbrush tool to select it and to bring to the front the Paintbrush Options floating palette. Click on the Brushes tab to bring it to the front. Choose Define brush from the pull-down menu.

4 The text you selected in Step 2 can now be used as a paintbrush. Press Delete to get rid of the original text. Deselect the rectangle. Next, with the Paintbrush tool still active and the new brush selected, click once in Layer 1. Keep clicking one stamp at a time to build your type.

180

TIP Just like all other Paint-
brushes, the stamp will be
applied in the current foreground color.

5 You also can click and drag the
word, but it probably will not be
readable because the letters will
blur together. To fix that problem,
double-click the brush you created
(on the Brushes floating palette).

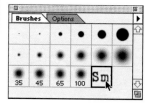

6 A dialog box will appear that
will enable you to change the
brush Spacing. The Spacing is the
distance the brush will move, relative to the vertical height of the
brush (the text), before placing
another stamp. Change the
Spacing to 100%.

7 Now try painting with the same
brush. See how you can make textures by simply dragging the type
brush and overlapping the words.

8 Click on the Paintbrush Options
tab to bring it to the front. Check
the Fade box to turn it on. Type a
number in the Fade box (I used
15), and set the steps to to
Transparent.

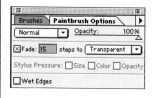

Then drag the same brush around.
After dragging the brush, I
changed the foreground color to
red and clicked on top of one of
the names.

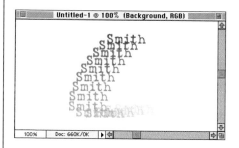

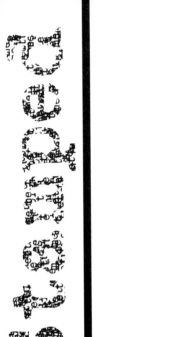

9 Try this. Open a file that has an image in it, like this one taken from the Photoshop Tutorial folder (Follow this path to find the Leaf image: Adobe Photoshop 4.0➡ Tutorial➡Leaf). Flatten the image to place it on a white background.

10 Change the foreground color to white, and paint the type over the photo to "mask" the image.

11 If it is not already active, click on the Paintbrush Options tab to bring it to the front. Then choose Exclusion from the pop-up menu.

12 Choose a color for the foreground color (other than white). I used a red from Photoshop's default swatches.

13 Next, click and drag the brush across the image.

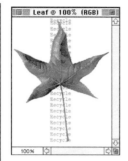

14 You could build type one letter at a time for a variation on the Binary effect (page 24). Do all the steps above as indicated, except select only one letter of the type in Step 2, and then do Step 3.

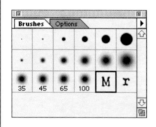

15 Repeat Step 14 until you have created a brush for each letter of the word.

16 Then use the brushes you have created to rebuild the word you typed.

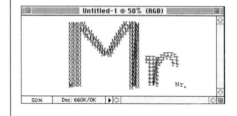

183

VARIATIONS

For this variation, type in several lines of type and then use the Marquee tool to select only a por-tion of the text.

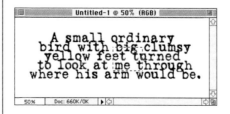

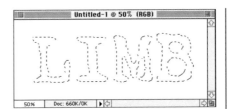

Define that selection as a brush, and change the brush spacing to 100% (as you did in Steps 5 and 6). Delete all the text. Then use the Type Mask tool to enter the text.

Change the foreground color to a color for the type. Select the Paintbrush tool again, and paint into the blank selection.

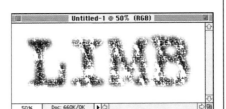

If you feather the selection above by choosing Select➛Feather (10 pixels) before you paint in the text, then you will get something like this.

Try making other brushes for painting type. I painted a paw, defined it as a brush, changed its spacing to 105%, and then painted this text.

184

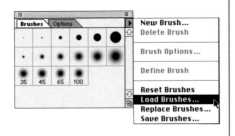

Try using one of the built-in brushes in Photoshop. From the Brushes floating palette arrow menu choose Load Brushes.

Find the Assorted Brushes file on your hard disk: Adobe Photoshop 4.0➡Goodies➡Brushes & Patterns➡Assorted Brushes. Open this file. You can use any of these brushes to paint your type. Don't forget that you can adjust the spacing for any of these brushes.

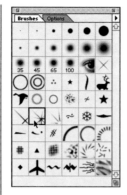

I made this image with the brush that was selected in the previous figure. ■

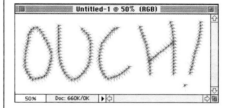

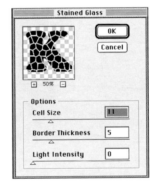

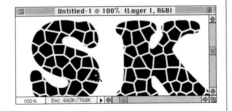

The new Stained Glass filter gets the Stones effect started by dividing up the letters. From there a little selection manipulation takes you to the Lighting Effects filter, which rounds out the stones and the effect.

1 Create a new file. Use the Type tool to enter the text. I used a thick font named Cooper Black at 100 points. The type will be placed automatically on a new layer (Layer 1).

2 Change the foreground color to white. Then choose Filter➔ Texture➔Stained Glass. Watch the preview to see the approximate sizes of the stones. Adjust the Border Thickness slider for spacing between the stones, and set the Light Intensity to 0. These settings...

...will yield this.

3 Select the Wand tool and click the wand inside one of the black spots.

4 Choose Select➔Similar. Save this selection to create Channel #4. Then choose Select➔Modify➔ Smooth. Smooth the selection about 3 pixels.

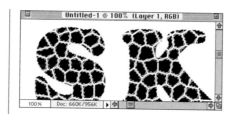

5 Press Command-J [Control-J] to float the smoothed selection into a new layer (Layer 2). Make Layer 1 invisible.

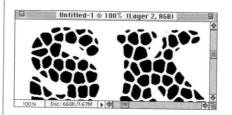

6 Turn on the Preserve Transparency option for Layer 2 on the Layers floating palette. Change the foreground color to black, and press the Option-Delete [Alt-Delete] keys to fill the layer with black. Then turn off the Preserve Transparency option. A few stones still may be attached to each other.

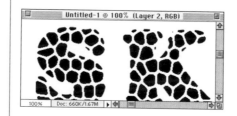

7 To get rid of these connections, load the selection Channel #4. Choose Select➔Inverse and press Delete.

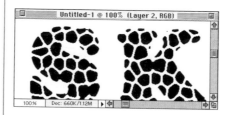

187

8 Next, duplicate Layer 2 to create Layer 2 copy. Then make Layer 2 the active layer again.

9 Select the Move tool and use the arrow keys to move this layer, which will be the shadow. I moved it two keystrokes to the right and two keystrokes down. It will look like the type is spreading in the direction you move it.

10 Then load the transparency selection for Layer 2 copy. Press Delete. You shouldn't see anything change, except for traces of white around the lower left of the stones.

11 Deselect the selection, and choose Filter➤Blur➤Gaussian Blur. Blur the shadow just a little, about 1 pixel.

12 Make Layer 2 copy active and load the transparency selection for this layer. Change the foreground color to 40% gray and fill the selection.

13 Save the selection to create Channel #5. Make Channel #5 active.

14 While the selection is still active, choose Filter➤Blur➤ Gaussian Blur. Raise the radius to about 6. Since the selection is active, there will be blurring only inside the white areas.

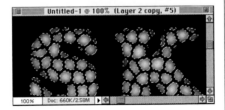

15 Return to the composite channel, and make Layer 2 copy the active layer.

16 Next, choose Filter➤Render➤ Lighting Effects. You can select the Stones preset from the pop-up menu or match these settings (which are very similar to the default settings). Move the light in the Preview box if necessary.

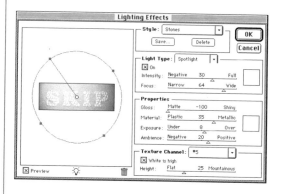

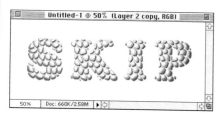

17 For the final touch, choose Filter➤Noise➤Add Noise. Adjust the Amount to your liking. I set it at 25, and turned on the Gaussian option. Turn the Monochromatic option on as well. ■

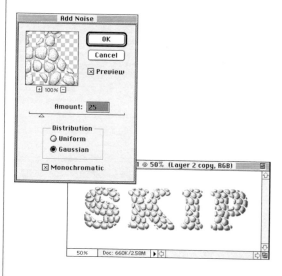

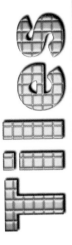

For this effect, I will show you two ways to create raised tiles. Some extra channel manipulation is needed to create tiles with hard, beveled edges, but first here's the easy way.

1 Create a new file, and a new channel (#4). Use the Type tool to enter the text. Use a wide font because narrow letter pieces will turn into awkward tile shapes. I used Eagle Book at 90 points.

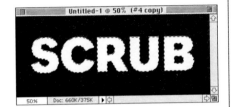

2 Duplicate Channel #4 to create Channel #4 copy.

3 While the selection is still active, choose Filter➔Stylize➔Tiles. The Number of Tiles setting is self-explanatory—choose a number that is appropriate for your type. Keep the Offset percentage at 1%.

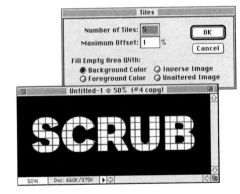

Tile (Lighting
Style Preset)

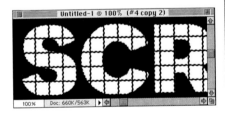

4 Duplicate Channel #4 copy to create Channel #4 copy 2.

5 Load the selection of the same channel (Channel #4 copy 2).

6 Choose Filter➤Blur➤Gaussian Blur. Blur the tiles just a little—about 2.5 pixels.

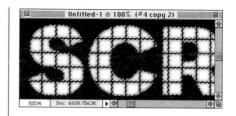

7 Next, choose Select➤Inverse. Then load the selection of Channel #4 with the Intersect with Selection option turned on. The grout should now be selected.

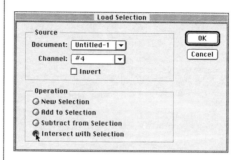

8 Blur the grout by choosing Filter➤Gaussian Blur. Use a smaller Radius than that used in Step 6. I set the Radius to 1.5.

9 Return to the composite channel, and load the selection Channel #4. Change the foreground color to a color for the type, and then fill the selection with the color. I used the CMYK values 50, 0, 0, 0.

191

10 Choose Filter➤Render➤ Lighting Effects. From the Style pop-up menu choose Tiles, or match the settings you see here.

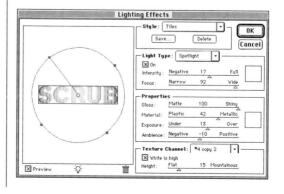

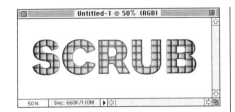

Easy tiles.

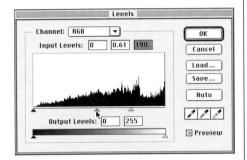

11 If you want to adjust the surface coverage of the color, then choose Image➤Adjust➤Levels. Use the Input Levels sliders to reduce or increase coverage and contrast. These adjustments...

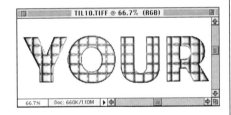

...yielded this type.

VARIATION

If you want harder edges, then follow these steps.

1 Perform Steps 1 through 4, and then deselect the text.

2 Choose Filter➤Blur➤Gaussian Blur and blur the channel about 1 pixel.

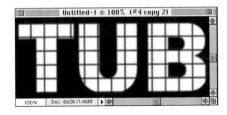

3 Duplicate Channel #4 copy 2 to create Channel #4 copy 3.

4 Then select the Move tool and nudge the channel one keystroke to the right and one keystroke down. Make Channel #4 copy 2 the active channel and nudge it one keystroke to the left and one keystroke up. This slight nudging sets up the next step.

5 Choose Image➤Calculations. Match your settings to the ones shown in this figure. This feature will create a new channel that is the result of combining Channel #4 copy 2 and Channel #4 copy 3. Because the channels are slightly offset, you get an interesting effect that helps create highlights on the tiles.

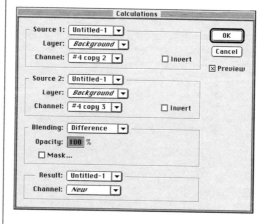

Click OK. The new channel (#8) should look like this.

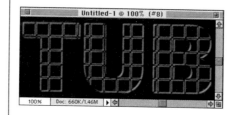

6 Choose Image➤Adjust➤Invert, and then Image➤Adjust➤Auto Levels. There should be more contrast in the type now.

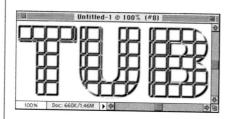

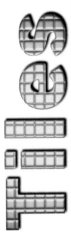

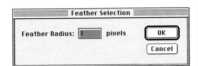

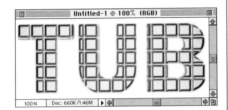

7 Return to the Composite channel, and load the selection (Channel #4 copy). Choose Select➛Feather (1 pixel).

8 Change the foreground color to a color for the tiles and fill the selection. Then choose Filter➛Render➛Lighting Effects. From the Style pop-up menu choose Tiles, or match the settings on page 191. Be sure to change the Texture Channel to Channel #8 in the Lighting Effects dialog box.

9 To add color to the grout, load the selection (Channel #4 copy), choose Select➛Inverse, and load the selection (Channel #4) with the Intersect with Selection option turned on. Choose a foreground color for the grout and fill the selection. I used the same color for the grout as I did for the tiles. ■

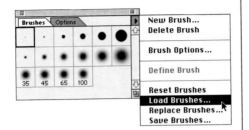

A custom paintbrush makes this effect a snap.

1 Create a new file. Double-click the Paintbrush tool to select and bring the Paintbrush Options floating palette to the front. Click the Brushes tab to make it active. Then, from the Brushes arrow menu, choose Load Brushes.

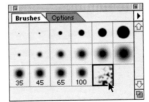

2 Find the Magic Brush file on the CD that came with this book. Follow this path to find the file: Photoshop Type Magic 2➤Type Magic Presets➤Magic Brush.

3 A new brush will appear at the end of the Brushes palette. I made this brush by modifying a brush from Photoshop's Assorted Brushes file. Select the new brush.

196

TOOLBOX

Magic Brush

Tire Tracks
(Lighting Style
Preset)

4 With the Paintbrush tool click and drag in the image window.

5 Simply draw your letters with the mouse.

VARIATIONS

If your hand is a little unsteady, or just want straighter lines, then try these steps.

Follow the instructions in Steps 1 through 3 above. Then select the Pen tool and use it to draw the center lines for the type. Like this:

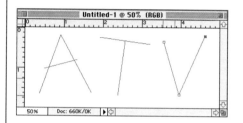

 Turning on the Rubber Band option on the Pen Tool Options floating palette helps you see what you're doing as you create the letters.

Now, from the Paths floating palette arrow menu, choose Stroke Path.

When the dialog box pops up, choose Paintbrush.

Click OK, and you have automatic tire tracks.

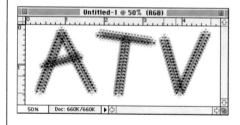

To add some depth to the tracks, follow these steps.

Double-click the new brush (the one that you selected in Step 3) to open the Brush Options dialog box. Set the Spacing at 35%.

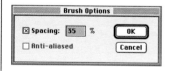

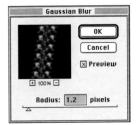

Create a new channel (#4), and draw the letters (as described above) in the channel.

Apply Filter➡Blur➡Gaussian Blur (Radius: 1.2 pixels).

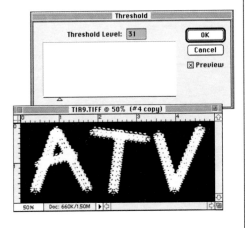

Duplicate Channel #4 to create Channel #4 copy. In the new channel, choose Image➡Adjust➡ Threshold. Lower the level until most of the text is white. I set the level at 30.

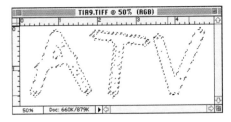

Return to the composite channel, and load the selection of Channel #4 copy. Choose Select➡Feather (1 pixel) to soften the edges.

198

Change the foreground color to a color for the tracks and fill the selection. The CMYK values for this color are 30, 59, 87, and 44.

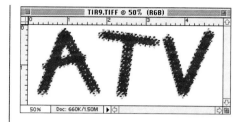

Choose Filter➟Render➟Lighting Effects. Use the Tire Tracks preset file or match these settings. ■

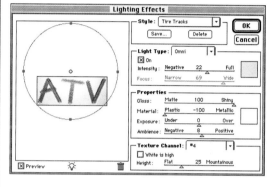

199

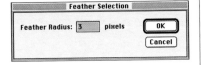

The type treatment for the frustrated. This technique is very easy, so don't let the number of steps intimidate you.

1 Create a new file, and a new channel (#4). Use the Type tool to enter the text. Something with a little weight will work best since part of the edges will diffuse into the tears. I used Bauhaus at 90 points.

2 Save the selection to create Channel #5.

3 Choose Select➡Modify➡ Contract. Contract the selection enough to create a good solid edge between the selection and the edge of the type. I chose 6 pixels.

4 Save the selection to create Channel #6. While still in Channel #4, load the selection Channel #4 to select the type. Then load the selection Channel #6 with Subtract from Selection option turned on. This is the selection you should now have.

5 Choose Select➡Feather and "feather" just a little. I chose 3 pixels.

6 Choose Filter➤Pixelate➤ Crystallize. Pick a medium Cell Size that ruffles the edge of the type similar to what you see in this figure. I chose 5 for my type.

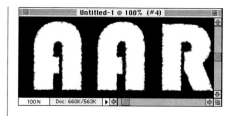

7 Next, choose Filter➤Noise➤Add Noise Set the Amount near 140. The edges will look like they are beginning to disintegrate.

8 Now choose Filter➤Noise➤ Median (1).

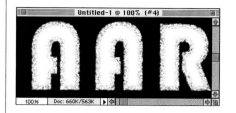

9 If you want rougher edges, keep the selection active and repeat Steps 6 (use Cell Size of 3) through 8 again. Otherwise, move on.

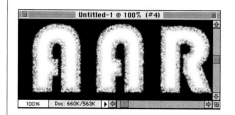

201

10 Choose Filter➤Noise➤Add Noise. Again, add just a small amount—about 40 pixels.

11 Deselect the type, and make Channel #5 active. Choose Filter➤Pixelate➤Crystallize. Choose a Cell Size similar to the Cell Size you used in Step 6. I chose 5.

12 Choose Image➤Adjust➤ Threshold, and slide the marker to the middle. I set the Threshold Level at 255.

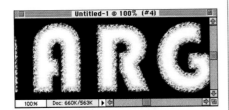

13 Make Channel #4 the active channel, then load the selection (Channel #5).

14 Choose Select➤Inverse, and fill the selection with black to harden the edges.

15 Choose Select➤Inverse again, and then choose Select➤Modify➤ Contract. Contract the selection the same amount as you did in Step 3.

16 Fill this selection with white to harden the inside edges.

17 Return to the composite channel, and make a new layer (Layer 1). Load the selection Channel #4.

18 Fill the selection with white. Nothing should happen in the image window because right now you have white on white.

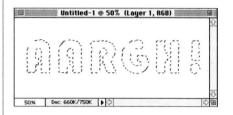

19 Make another layer (Layer 2), then move that layer below Layer 1.

20 The selection should still be active. Change the foreground color to black. Choose Select➡ Feather and feather the selection just one pixel.

21 Fill the selection with black.

22 Select the Move tool and use the arrow keys to move the selection one or two keystrokes to the right and one or two keystrokes down.

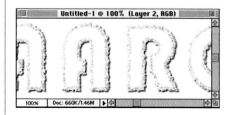

23 That's the type.

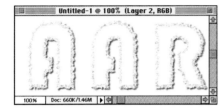

TIP If you want to soften the contrast, use the Opacity slider
on the Layers palette for
Layer 2. ■

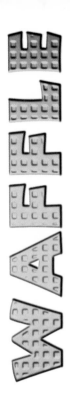

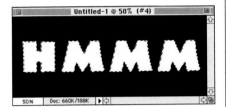

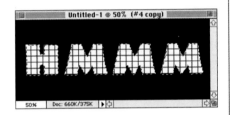

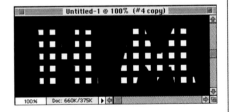

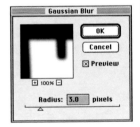

A few fancy selections serve up
this delicious effect.

1 Create a new file, and a new
channel (#4). Use the Type tool to
enter text into the new channel:
the bigger the font, the bigger the
waffle. The fattest font I had was
Informal Black (80 points).

2 Make a copy of Channel #4 to
create Channel #4 copy. Choose
Filter➤Stylize➤Tiles. The first setting in this filter will determine
scale of the pancake grid. I set the
Number of Tiles to 5. Keep the
Maximum offset percentage at 1
to keep everything in line.

3 Choose Select➤Modify➤Expand
(1 pixel). Apply Filter➤Other➤
Minimum (Radius: 5). These commands build the hollows. Deselect
the text.

4 Make another copy of Channel
#4. You should now be in
Channel #4 copy 2. Choose
Filter➤Blur➤Gaussian Blur
(Radius: 3).

5 Load the selection Channel #4 copy, and choose Select➔ Modify➔Smooth (1 pixel). Then Select➔Feather (2 pixels). Change the foreground color to a medium gray. Fill the selection, and then deselect it.

6 Return to the composite channel, and load the selection Channel #4. Choose Select➔ Modify➔Expand (1 pixel), and Select➔Modify➔Smooth (1 pixel).

7 Change the foreground color to the CMYK values 11, 15, 70, 2. Fill the selection with this color.

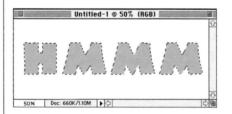

8 Choose Filter➔Render➔Lighting Effects. Click on the Style pop-up menu and find the Waffle preset. If you haven't loaded the presets from the CD, then you can match the settings you see here. Don't forget the Texture channel.

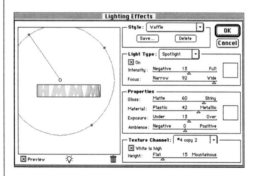

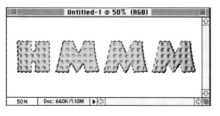

207

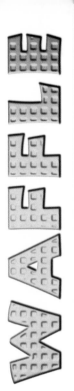

9 Put down that fork, there is still one more touch. Keep the selection active, and select the Marquee tool. Move the selection using the arrow keys. Press the right arrow and down arrow keys two times each. I am setting up a selection for a shadow.

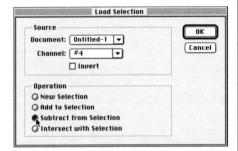

10 Load the selection Channel #4 (the original text channel), but choose the Subtract from Selection option in the Load Selection dialog box. The part of the selection that was on top of the letters is cut out.

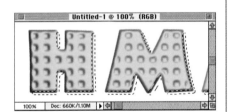

11 Next, choose Select➡Feather (2 pixels). Again, use the arrow keys to move the selection. Up one keystroke and left one keystroke.

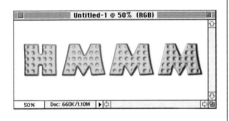

12 Change the foreground color to 70% gray, and fill the selection. Deselect the text, and pour on the syrup.

VARIATIONS

Okay, so you probably wouldn't eat these. Load the selection Channel #4 copy, and choose Image➡Adjust➡Hue/Saturation. Turn on the Colorize option and use the markers to change the color of the hollows. Then load the selection Channel #4 copy 2, and change the color of the rest of the type in the same way.

Follow the variation above, but choose Filter➡Stylize➡Find Edges, rather than changing the colors in the selections.

To make lead waffles, load the selection Channel #4, and choose Filter➡Other➡High Pass. I set the Radius in this example to 12 pixels. ■

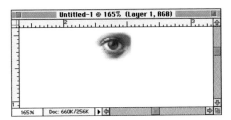

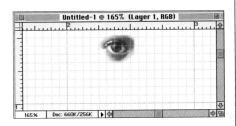

The new Grid feature in Photoshop 4.0 helps make a "seamless" pattern to fill this text.

1 Create a new file. Change the foreground color to a color for the background. Fill the Background layer with this color. I left it white.

2 Make a new layer (Layer 1).

3 You can draw any image you want for the wallpaper pattern. I loaded the Assorted Brushes file into the Brushes palette and used the eye paintbrush.

TIP Don't forget that you can define your own brush using an image that you have created. See your Photoshop user manual to find out how to define a brush.

4 Change the Foreground color to 80% black, and click in the image area with the eye paintbrush.

5 Choose View➔Show Grid, and then choose File➔Preferences➔ Guides and Grid. Change the Subdivisions amount to something that divides your image into four or five boxes in either direction. The grid will change as you try different Subdivision values. I set it at 16. After clicking OK, choose View➔Snap to Grid.

6 Select the Move tool and move the image until the upper-left part of the image locks into a corner of the grid.

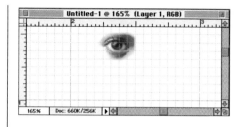

7 Duplicate Layer 1 (Layer 1 copy). Use the Move tool and move the image to the right and down any distance that you like. As you move the image, let it bounce from gridline to gridline. Keep track of the number of lines you move the image. I moved this image four lines to the right and two down.

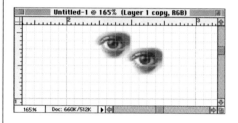

8 Choose Layer➡Merge Down to press the two eyes together into Layer 1. Layer 1 copy will merge into Layer 1, so you can duplicate Layer 1 again to create a new Layer 1 copy.

9 Use the Move tool and move the image the same number of gridlines down as in Step 7. Also, move the image the same number of gridlines to the left as you moved it to the right in Step 7. Choose Layer➡Merge Down.

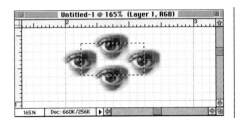

10 Choose View➡Snap to Grid to turn off the grid snap. Select the Marquee tool and drag a selection like the one shown in the figure. It is very important that the top of the selection runs through the top image in the same place as the bottom of the selection runs through the bottom image. Treat the left and right edges of the selection in the same way.

11 Choose Edit➡Define Pattern to set this selection as the wallpaper pattern. Deselect the selection.

12 Delete Layer 1. Fill the Background layer with white (if it isn't already). Turn off the grid by choosing View➡Hide Grid.

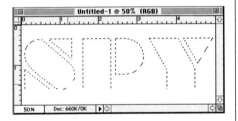

13 Then use the Type Mask tool to enter the text. Use something like Braggadocio that has a lot of room for the pattern (120 points).

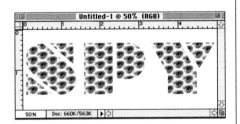

14 Choose Edit➡Fill, and then choose Pattern from the Contents pop-up menu.

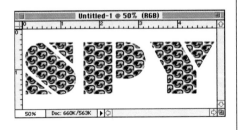

15 I couldn't resist a filter. I applied Filter➡Stylize➡Find Edges.

VARIATIONS

You also can make an arrangement of images, like this...

...into a pattern using the same
steps listed previously. Just treat
the arrangement as if it were a
single image.

If you make the Background layer
invisible before Step 11, then you
can define a pattern with a transparent background. This enables
you to place a pattern over type
you have already created—like this
type that already has a texture.

Photoshop contains a set of seamless patterns that you can use to
make wallpaper. Follow this path
to find the PostScript Patterns
folder: Adobe Photoshop 4.0➡
Goodies➡Brushes and Patterns➡
Postcript Patterns.Choose one of
the patterns to open. I opened the
Mali primitive file.If the Rasterize
Generic EPS Format dialog box
opens, click OK to accept the values it provides for the settings.

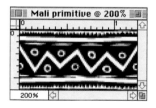

Choose Select➡All, and then
choose Edit➡Define Pattern.
Close the file, create a new file
and follow the instruction in Steps
13 and 14. I also colorized the
image (Image➡Adjust➡Hue
/Saturation). ■

213

This effect uses the Median filter to blur colored areas together. It works much better in an RGB file than a CMYK file because of the brighter RGB gamut.

1 Create a new file. Use the Type tool to enter the text. MetaPlus-Black at 100 points was used for this effect. The type will be placed automatically on a new layer (Layer 1).

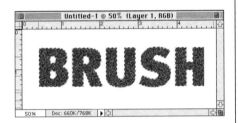

2 Load the selection Layer 1 Transparency. To break up the flat color and to add some new colors, choose Filter➤Noise➤Add Noise. I set the Amount at 600.

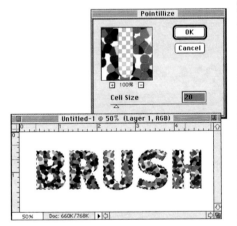

3 Choose Filter➤Pixelate➤Pointillize. Choose a medium-to-large Cell Size. I used 20. Find a Cell Size that fits your type like this.

214

4 The black areas in the type will take away from the watercolor look. To get rid of them, choose Image➤Adjust➤Replace Color. Now get the eyedropper in the dialog box and click a black dot in the image window.

5 Use the Fuzziness slider to control how much of the other blacks are selected. If the Selection button is on, then the white areas represent the areas that will be affected by changing the sliders below. If you set the Fuzziness to high, then when you change the black in the next step you may also change some of the other colors. So, set the Fuzziness high enough to select as much black as possible without affecting the other colors very much.

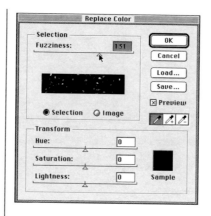

 TIP You will still be able to adjust the Fuzziness setting after moving the markers in the next step.

6 To change the blacks to another color, slide the Saturation marker all the way to the right. Then use the Hue and Lightness markers to find a new color.

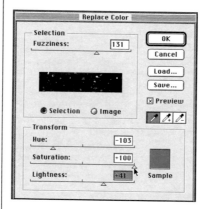

215

7 Choose Filter➔Noise➔Median. This filter is going to blend and overlap the dots made with the Pointillize filter. Play with the setting. This image was made by setting the Radius to 14.

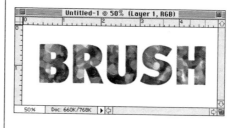

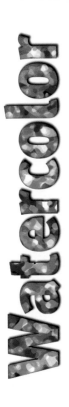

VARIATIONS

Variations abound for this effect. Here are two minor variations that you may prefer to the hard-edged type above.

1 Complete all of the steps above, then choose Layer➤Merge Down. Deselect the text. Choose Filter➤Noise➤Median again and use a low setting to smooth the edges of the type. I used a Radius of 6 for this image.

2 After Step 3, choose Layer➤Merge Down. After you complete the rest of the steps, your type will look something like this.

Here are some other variations that are take-offs from the steps above.

3 Do Steps 1 through 7. Then choose Filter➤Stylize➤Find Edges to turn the seeping-color spots into lines.

Then choose Filter➤Other➤Minimum. You probably will not want to use a Radius higher than 1 or 2. If you do then the lines will blur together as they become dark and thick.

4 Keep going. Again, choose Filter➤Stylize➤Find Edges to build patterns into the type.

5 For a variation of that variation, choose Layer➤Merge Down after Step 7, and deselect the text. Then do the steps for Variations 3 and 4.

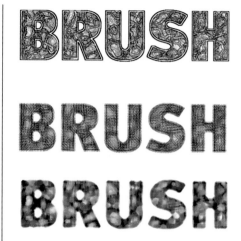

6 Do the steps for Variations 3 and 4 and try this: choose Filter➤Pixelate➤Fragment to get some funky patterns.

7 Instead of applying the Fragment filter above, choose Merge➤Down. Then choose our friend Filter➤Noise➤Median. For this image I used a Radius of 6.

8 If you use colored type in Step 1 and choose a low noise value such as 50 in Step 2, then completing the rest of the steps will give you something like this. ■

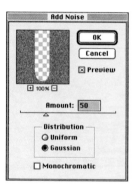

For this woven effect, you need to create the texture first, and then turn it into type.

1 Create a new file. Double-click the Marquee tool to select it and make the Marquee Options floating palette active. Make sure that you have selected the rectangular Marquee tool.

2 Change the Style to Fixed Size. The Width and Height dimensions determine the size of the weave. Enter the same number for both dimensions. I used 15 pixels.

3 Zoom in to any area of the blank image area. I zoomed in to 300%. With the Marquee tool click once in the image area. Fill the square selection with black.

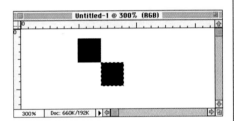

4 Then move the selection, with the Marquee tool, until the upper-left corner of the selection meets the lower-right corner of the black square. Fill the selection with black.

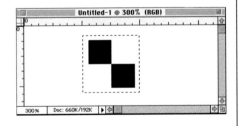

5 Find the Marquee Options floating palette again and change the Style back to Normal. Drag a selection to encompass both black squares.

6 Then choose Layer➥Transform➥ Numeric and enter 45° in the Rotate box. Turn off the Position, Scale, and Skew options.

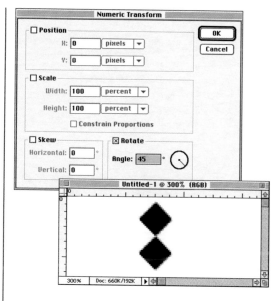

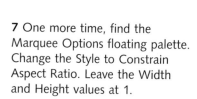

7 One more time, find the Marquee Options floating palette. Change the Style to Constrain Aspect Ratio. Leave the Width and Height values at 1.

8 Click and drag the Marquee tool to make a selection like this.

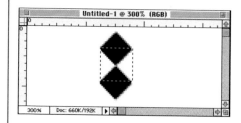

9 Choose Edit➥Define Pattern. Nothing happens, but the active selection has been saved as a pattern.

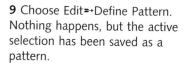

219

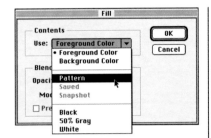

10 Choose Select➔All, and then choose Edit➔Fill. Change the Contents option to Pattern. Deselect the selection.

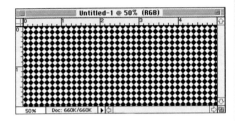

Click OK.

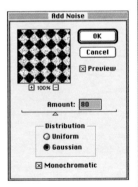

11 Add a little noise to the checkers by choosing Filter➔Noise➔ Add Noise. I set the Amount at 80. Turn on the Monochromatic option. The noise helps the next filter do its job.

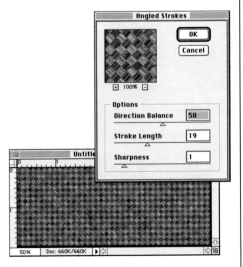

12 Apply Filter➔Brush Strokes➔ Angled Strokes. Use these settings: Direction Balance, 50; Stroke Length, 19; and Sharpness, 1.

13 Now, we need some type. Use the Type Mask tool to enter the text. This font is Seagull Heavy at 100 points.

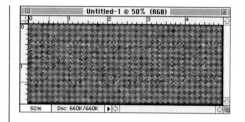

14 Choose Select➤Inverse and press Delete.Then choose Select➤ Inverse again to select the type.

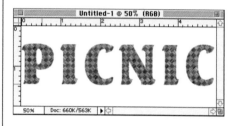

15 To add some color, choose Image➤Adjust➤Hue/Saturation. Now turn on the Colorize option and find a color for the texture.

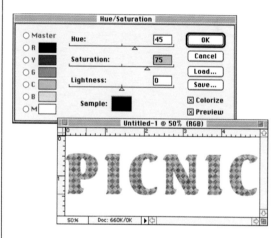

16 For some fine-tuning, choose Image➤Adjust➤Levels. Use the Input markers to adjust the values in the weave. I set the Input markers at 21, 0.88, and 255. For extra contrast, click the Auto button. ■

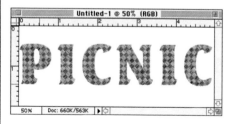

221

Appendix A

Contributor's Listing

The following companies have provided the software, filters, and stock photography for the CD-ROM that is included with this book. For more information on their products, use the contact information listed here.

Filters

Alien Skin Software

2522 Clark Avenue

Raleigh, NC 27607

voice: 919/832-4124

fax: 919/832-4065

email: alienskin@aol.com

On the CD: Cutout filter demo

Andromeda Software

699 Hampshire Road, Suite 109

Westlake Village

Thousand Oaks, CA 91361

voice: 805/379-4109, 800/547-0055

fax: 805/379-5253

email: andromeda@aol.com

On the CD: Series 1-4 filters demo

MetaTools, Inc.

6303 Carpinteria Avenue

Carpinteria, CA 93013

voice: 805/566-6200

fax: 805/566-6385

web: http://www.metatools.com

On the CD: KPT filter hub demo

Xaos Tools, Inc.

600 Townsend Street, Suite 270 East

San Francisco, CA 94103

voice: 415/487-7000, 800/289-9267

fax: 415/558-9886

email: macinfo@xaostools.com

On the CD: Terrazo, Paint Alchemy, Typecaster demos

Software

Adobe Systems Incorporated

345 Park Avenue

San Jose, CA 95110-2704

voice: 408/536-6000

fax: 408/537-6000

web: http://www.adobe.com

On the CD: Acrobat Reader, After Effects, Dimensions, Illustrator, Photoshop, Premiere, Streamline, TextureMaker demos

Affinity Microsystems Ltd.

934 Pearl Street, Suite H

Boulder, CO 80302

voice: 800/367-6771

fax: 303/442-4999

On the CD: TempoEZ demo

Equilibrium

475 Gate Five Road, Suite 225

Sausalito, CA 94965

voice: 800/524-8651, 415/332-4343

fax: 415/332-4433

On the CD: DeBabelizer lite (full working version), DeBabelizer demo

Jawai Interactive

501 E. Fourth Street, #511

Austin, TX 78701

voice: 512/469-0502

email: jawai@aol.com

On the CD: Screen Caffeine Pro demo, Java Beat demo

Macromedia, Incorporated

600 Townsend Street

San Francisco, CA 94103

voice: 415/252-2000

fax: 415/626-0554

web: http://macromedia.com

On the CD: Director, Fontographer, xRes demos

MicroFrontier

P.O. Box 71190

Des Moines, IA 50322

voice: 515/270-8109, 800/388-8109

fax: 515/278-6828

email: Mfrontier@aol.com

On the CD: ColorIt demo, plus patterns

225

Specular

479 West Street

Amherst, MA 01002

voice: 413/253-3100, 800/433-7732

fax: 413/253-0540

email: specular@applelink.apple.com

web: http://www.specular.com

On the CD: InifiD, LogoMotion, TextureScape demos

Images

PhotoDisc Inc.

2013 Fourth Avenue

Fourth Floor

Seattle, WA 98121

voice: 206/441-9355, 800/528-3472

fax: 206/441-9379

web: http://www.photodisc.com

Image Club Graphics

729 Twenty-Fourth Avenue, SE

Calgary, AB CANADA

T2G 5K8

voice: 403/262-8008, 800/661-9410

fax: 403/261-7013

web: http://www.adobe.com/imageclub

Used with express permission.

Adobe® and Image Club Graphics™

are trademarks of Adobe Systems

Incorporated.

Digital Stock

400 S. Sierra Avenue, Suite 100

Solana Beach, CA 92075-2262

voice: 619/794-4040, 800/545-4514

fax: 619/794-4041

web: http://www.digitalstock.com

D'Pix

Division of Amber Productions

414 W. Fourth Avenue

Columbus, OH 43201

voice: 614/299-7192

fax: 614/294-0002

Appendix B

What's on the CD-ROM

The CD-ROM included with this book is full of filters, images, and software applications for you to try. It is also where you will find the special preset files to be used with the effects described in this book.

The CD-ROM that comes with this book is both Macintosh and Windows CD-ROM compatible. Please note: There are several demos and tryouts available for Macintosh users that are not available for Windows users, and vice versa. This means one of two things: either the product has not been created for that platform, or a version of the product is being created but is not yet completed.

I suggest that you refer to the READ ME and other information files which are included in the demo software program's folder. Also, visit the corporate Web sites; the URLs are noted in the Contributors Listing (Appendix A). There are often demos of new software available for downloading and tryout.

The contents of the CD-ROM are divided into four folders: Type Magic Presets, Filters, Software, and Images. The following is a brief description of the folder contents.

Type Magic Presets

Inside the Type Magic Presets folder you will find another folder named Lighting Presets. This folder contains 22 Lighting Style presets to be used with Photoshop's Lighting Effects filter. Proper installation of these files is critical. In order to use these files, they must be copied from the CD-ROM into the Lighting Styles folder within the Adobe Photoshop folder on your hard drive. Follow this path to find the proper folder: Adobe Photoshop 4.0➡Plug-ins➡Filters➡Lighting FX➡Lighting Styles. After copying these files, the next time you start Photoshop they will appear in the Style list in the Lighting Effects dialog box.

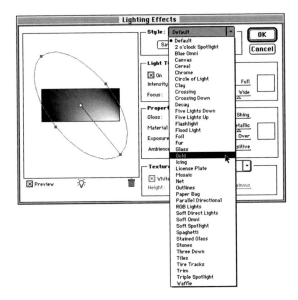

There is one more file in the Type Magic Presets folder. This file, Magic Brush, contains a custom paintbrush to be used in the Canvas and Tire Tracks effects. If you want, you can leave this file on the CD and simply access it when needed. You also can copy it to the folder that contains the Photoshop brushes files. Follow this path to find the folder: Adobe Photoshop 4.0➡Goodies➡Brushes and Patterns. Copy the file to the Brushes and Patterns folder.

Filters

Inside the Filters folder are four folders. Each of these folders, named for the software companies that created the filters, contain demo filters that you can test on your type and other images. To use any of these filters, they need to be copied into the Plug-ins folder inside the Adobe Photoshop 4.0 folder on your hard drive. Follow this path to copy the files: Adobe Photoshop 4.0➡Plug-ins. The next time you start Photoshop, these third-party filter demos will appear at the bottom of the Filter menu. For example:

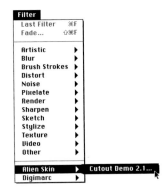

These filters appear on the CD:

KPT Filter Hub, Full demo

Black Box Cutout filter demo

Andromeda Series 1-4 demo

Terrazo demo

Paint Alchemy demo

Typecaster demo

Software

Inside this folder are demo versions of popular software applications that you can try. For detailed information about how to install and run these applications, consult the READ ME files that are contained within the individual folders. Each folder contains an installation file that walks you through the installation of the software.

These applications appear on the CD:

Adobe Acrobat Reader

Adobe After Effects

Adobe Dimensions

Adobe Illustrator

Adobe Photoshop

Adobe Premiere

Adobe Streamline

ColorIt

InfiniD

LogoMotion

TextureScape

DeBabelizer

DeBabelizer Lite (full working versions)

Director

Fontographer

FreeHand

xRes

Power/Pac 1

Sample output from Adobe TextureMaker

TempoEZ

Images

Inside the Images folder are four folders that contain a variety of low, medium, and high resolution stock photography images. Many of the images contain textures and backgrounds that can be used to make great-looking type. Most likely you will decide to keep these images on the CD, where you can access them at will—without having them eat up memory on your hard drive. (If you wish, they also may be moved to your hard drive.) All of these images can be opened with the Open command in Adobe Photoshop.

These companies have provided images for the CD:

Digital Stock

D'Pix

Image Club Graphics

PhotoDisc

Gallery

page 18

CARPET

page 38

page 24

Cereal

page 40

Camouflage

page 28

Checkered

page 44

Canvas

page 32

page 50

page 54

page 58

page 60

page 66

page 72

page 74

page 78

page 84

Foil

page 88

Highlights

page 102

FONTS

page 90

page 106

FUR

page 96

LICENSE PLATE

page 112

GOLD

page 100

LIGHTS

page 114

MARBLE

page 120

PAPER BAG

page 138

MARQUEE

page 122

Pinched

page 142

Mosaic

page 126

Plaid

page 144

NET

page 132

Reflector

page 148

SCRAPS

page 152

STAINED GLASS

page 172

SCRIBBLE

page 158

Stamped

page 180

SHAPING

page 162

Stones

page 186

Shimmering

page 168

Tiles

page 190

TIRE TRACKS

page 196

Watercolor

page 214

TORN PAPER

page 200

Woven

page 218

WAFFLE

page 206

WALLPAPER

page 210

Other DESIGN/GRAPHICS Titles

Designing Business

Provides the design/business communities with a new way of thinking about how the right design can be a strategic business advantage. It is the definitive guide to presenting a business identity through the use of traditional media vehicles and emerging technologies.

- CD-ROM (dual-platform) exhibits interactive prototypes of multimedia brochures, interactive television, and Web sites as developed by Clement Mok Designs Inc., one of the most sought after interactive design agencies in the world
- Shows how effective communication is one way to out-think, out-plan, and out-perform the competition

Clement Mok
1-56830-282-7 ▪ $60.00 USA/$81.95 CDN
264 pp., 8 x 10, Covers PC and Macintosh, New - Expert
Available Now

Adobe Persuasion: Classroom in a Book
1-56830-316-5 ▪ $40.00 USA/$56.95 CDN
Available November 1996

Learning Adobe FrameMaker
1-56830-290-8 ▪ $60.00 USA/$81.95 CDN
Available Now

Adobe Illustrator for Windows: Classroom in a Book
1-56830-053-0 ▪ $44.95 USA/$59.99 CDN
Available Now

Adobe Pagemaker for Windows: Classroom in a Book
1-56830-184-7 ▪ $45.00 USA/$61.95 CDN
Available Now

Adobe Photoshop: Classroom in a Book
1-56830-317-3 ▪ $45.00 USA/$63.95 CDN
Available Now

Advanced Adobe PageMaker for Windows 95: Classroom in a Book
1-56830-262-2 ▪ $50.00 USA/$68.95 CDN
Available Now

Advanced Adobe Photoshop for Windows: Classroom in a Book
1-56830-116-2 ▪ $50.00 USA/$68.95 CDN
Available Now

The Amazing PhotoDeluxe Book for Windows
1-56830-286-X ▪ $30.00 USA/$40.95 CDN
Available Now

Branding with Type
1-56830-248-7 ▪ $18.00 USA/$24.95 CDN
Available Now

The Complete Guide to Trapping, Second Edition
1-56830-098-0 ▪ $30.00 USA/$40.95 CDN
Available Now

Design Essentials, Second Edition
1-56830-093-X ▪ $40.00 USA/$54.95 CDN
Available Now

Digital Type Design Guide
1-56830-190-1 ▪ $45.00 USA/$61.95 CDN
Available Now

Fractal Design Painter Creative Techniques
1-56830-283-5 ▪ $40.00 USA/$56.95 CDN
Available Now

Photoshop Type Magic 1
1-56830-220-7 ▪ $35.00 USA/$47.95 CDN
Available Now

Photoshop Web Magic
1-56830-314-9 ▪ $45.00 USA/$63.95 CDN
Available November 1996

Adobe Photoshop Complete
1-56830-323-8 ▪ $45.00 USA/$61.95 CDN
Available Now

Production Essentials
1-56830-124-3 ▪ $40.00 USA/$54.95 CDN
Available Now

Stop Stealing Sheep & find out how type works
0-672-48543-5 ▪ $19.95 USA/$26.99 CDN
Available Now

Visit your fine local bookstore, or for more information visit us at http//:www.mcp.com/hayden

REGISTRATION CARD

Photoshop Type Magic 2

Hayden
Books

Name _____ Title _____

Company_____Type of business _____

Address _____

City/State/ZIP _____

Have you used these types of books before? ☐ yes ☐ no

If yes, which ones? _____

_____

How many computer books do you purchase each year? ☐ 1–5 ☐ 6 or more

How did you learn about this book?_____

    ☐ recommended by a friend ☐ received ad in mail

    ☐ recommended by store personnel ☐ read book review

    ☐ saw in catalog ☐ saw on bookshelf

Where did you purchase this book? _____

Which applications do you currently use? _____

Which computer magazines do you subscribe to? _____

What trade shows do you attend? _____

Please number the top three factors which most influenced your decision for this book purchase.

    ☐ cover ☐ price

    ☐ approach to content ☐ author's reputation

    ☐ logo ☐ publisher's reputation

    ☐ layout/design ☐ other _____

Would you like to be placed on our preferred mailing list? ☐ yes ☐ no e-mail address _____

☐ **I would like to see my name in print!** You may use my name and quote me in future Hayden products and promotions. My daytime phone number is: _____

Comments _____

_____

_____

Hayden Books Attn: Product Marketing ◆ 201 West 103rd Street ◆ Indianapolis, Indiana 46290 USA

Fax to **317-581-3576** Visit out Web Page **http://WWW.MCP.com/hayden/**

Fold Here

- -

BUSINESS REPLY MAIL

FIRST-CLASS MAIL PERMIT NO. 9918 INDIANAPOLIS IN

POSTAGE WILL BE PAID BY THE ADDRESSEE

HAYDEN BOOKS
Attn: Product Marketing
201 W 103RD ST
INDIANAPOLIS IN 46290-9058

Other INTERNET Titles

Creating Killer Web Sites

The book has an accompanying Web site, where visitors can see the pages in action, download the code for their favorite designs, see tutorials and examples not found in the book, and interact with the author. An estimated 100,000 Web site designers are hungry for this information; by August of 1996, their number was expected to double.

- Conferences about designing for the Internet are selling out, and designers are challenged as they make the transition from print to new media design
- Written by one of today's most noted Web designers
- The first book to teach the art as well as the craft of site design

David Siegel
1-56830-289-4 ■ $45.00 USA/$63.95 CDN

272 pp., 8 x 10, Covers PC and Macintosh, Accomplished - Expert
Available Now

Advertising on the Web: Planning & Design Strategies
1-56830-310-6 ■ $40.00 USA/$56.95 CDN
Available October 1996

Macromedia Shockwave for Director
1-56830-275-4 ■ $30.00 USA/$40.95 CDN
Available Now

Photoshop Web Magic
1-56830-314-9 ■ $45.00 USA/$63.95 CDN
Available November 1996

Virtus VRML Toolkit
1-56830-247-9 ■ $40.00 USA/$54.95 CDN
Available Now

Designer's Guide to the Internet
1-56830-229-0 ■ $30.00 USA/$40.95 CDN
Available Now

Internet Starter Kit for Windows 95
1-56830-260-6 ■ $35.00 USA/$47.95 CDN
Available Now

Internet Starter Kit for Windows, Second Edition
1-56830-177-4 ■ $30.00 USA/$40.95 CDN
Available Now

The Adobe PageMill 2.0 Handbook
1-56830-313-0 ■ $40.00 USA/$56.95 CDN
Available Now

Designing Multimedia Web Sites
1-56830-308-4 ■ $50.00 USA/$70.95 CDN
Available Now

Designing Animation for the Web
1-56830-309-2 ■ $40.00 USA/$56.95 CDN
Available Now

Designing Interactivity for the Web: How to Keep People Coming Back
1-56830-311-4 ■ $50.00 USA/$70.95 CDN
Available Now

Internet Publishing with Adobe Acrobat
1-56830-300-9 ■ $40.00 USA/$56.95 CDN
Available Now

Kids do the Web
1-56830-315-7 ■ $25.00 USA/$35.95 CDN
Available Now

Style Sheets for the Web
1-56830-306-8 ■ $35.00 USA/$49.95 CDN
Available Now

Web Page Scripting Techniques: JavaScript, VBScript, and Advanced HTML
1-56830-307-6 ■ $50.00 USA/$70.95 CDN
Available Now

World Wide Web Design Guide
1-56830-171-5 ■ $40.00 USA/$54.95 CDN
Available Now

Adobe PageMill 2.0: Classroom in a Book
1-56830-319-X ■ $40.00 USA/$56.95 CDN
Available Now

Visit your fine local bookstore, or for more information visit us at http//:www.mcp.com/hayden